Bags with Style

Stephanie Kimura

Acknowledgments

This book is for you and I hope it entices you to start sewing, come back to sewing, or keep on sewing. If you don't know where to start or just want creative friends, join the American Sewing Guild (www.asg.org) or visit your local fabric and quilt shops.

I would like to thank Christine Townsend, my editor, who went above and beyond the call of her duties to help me create this wonderful book. I am grateful to the Krause team (most notably: editor Maria Turner, cover and page designer Marilyn McGrane, photographers Bob Best and Kris Kandler, sales representative Brenda Mazemke, acquisitions editor Julie Stephani, and page designer Jan Wojtech), Sandra Millett, my students who always teach me something, Pat and Mark of the Sewing Studio who made all the supplies available to me, and all the companies on the resource list.

©2004 Stephanie Kimura

Published by

kp krause publications
An F+W Publications Company

700 East State Street • Iola, WI 54990-0001
715-445-2214 • 888-457-2873
www.krause.com

Our toll-free number to place an order or obtain a free catalog is (800) 258-0929.

Library of Congress Catalog Number: 2003115661
ISBN: 0-87349-740-6

Edited by Christine Townsend and Maria Turner
Designed by Marilyn McGrane and Jan Wojtech

Printed in the United States of America

Chapter 4: Projects 28

Introduction

Bags with style have been a big part of my life, and if you're like me, shoes have been, too. These two accessories have been friends for decades. My first bag held lollipops and pennies, and had pink bows that matched my strappy shoes. As I grew, the bags kept getting bigger to carry more important things like quarters (which rolled around on the bottom), books, and pencils. Of course, my shoes got bigger, but I abandoned the Mary Janes in favor of sneakers. As time and fashions changed, the bags I carried got cute again, and I began coordinating them with high heels. Now, the passing decades make me ask, "Can I run for a cab while tottering in these shoes?" I may be in doubt about shoes now, but my friendship with bags continues unbroken because they always fit, they are quick and easy to make, and they make me happy.

The bags in this book are versatile. The same pattern can create a bag for different seasons just by changing the fabric, color, or handle. They can be made in different sizes by reducing or enlarging the pattern. The same bag can be made for an elegant evening or a casual lunch just by changing the embellishment or making it reversible.

Create fantasy without leaving your sewing room! Fashion a bag using African fabrics for a safari or embellish one with ancient Asian coins and listen for the chimes of the Far East. Use a strand of fluffy feathers on a bag to carry your paperback Parisian romance, or attach sturdy cargo pockets onto a canvas bag to trek the sales at the mall. Whatever your fantasy, these friends are always ready and willing to go along.

Table of Contents

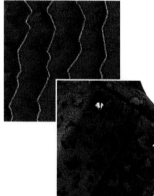

Chapter 4: Projects 28

chapter 1

Selecting the Elements

You may be wondering which purse to make first, or which purse you could alter to make your very own. The inspiration for such decisions can come from anywhere: a special event looming on the horizon; a button from an antique shop; a fabric find marked 70 percent off; or some handles or bangles you bought from a vendor at a festival.

Once you have your inspiration piece, it's time to head to your stash of fabrics, threads, and embellishments. Start pulling out fabrics, opening boxes of thread, jars of buttons, plastic bags of trims, and peruse the projects in this book for ideas.

Fabric will be an important beginning. The choice of fabric will depend upon your inspiration. Select a fabric suitable for the occasion or your ensemble, and the bag becomes the perfect accessory. Look through the following chapters and become acquainted with the variety of fabrics available to you. Feel free to mix cottons with silks and fur with leather. Make a reversible bag and you've actually made two: one side casual cottons and the other side sexy silk.

Because there are always new fabric designs available, you may not be able to exactly duplicate the book's samples; however, choosing fabrics with the same "feel" will produce similar results. With different color and fabric selections, the finished projects will carry your individual stamp of creativity.

Get organized. Create an area where your bag findings can be grouped together. Look through the checklist of equipment, tools, and fabrics needed for the chosen project. Gather together what is in your stash and make a list of what is needed. Become familiar with the terms that will be used. Read about the kinds of battings to see which is appropriate for a specific project. If you are not sure, cut swatches of fabric and batting and test them with decorative threads.

Your sewing machine should be in good working order. Clean and oil your machine, and check the tension. Confirm that you have the sewing machine feet and needles required for the project. Basic attachments such as the standard sewing foot and the satin stitch foot are essential. If your machine has "darning" or "free-motion" capability, either will allow you more freedom in the selection of quilting designs. If you do not have free-motion capability, then quilt with straight stitches using angular lines.

You will need pins, hand sewing needles, a seam ripper, washable or erasable markers, and a tape measure. A good, sharp pair of scissors is important for cutting fabrics, but use only craft scissors for cutting patterns. A rotary cutter, mat, and ruler will help to cut accurate strips. Invest in a good iron and a Teflon® pressing sheet.

These optional sewing aids can make the project go faster with more accuracy. A Fasturn® can turn tubes inside out in seconds. A mini iron (Clover® makes a nice one) can reach into tight corners and allows you to press small areas without setting up the ironing board.

Hand-painted silk scarves can be transformed into a one-of-a-kind purse.

fabrics

With so many fabrics from which to choose, you may have a difficult time deciding. Here are a few points to consider: Although one good thing about selecting fabrics for your bag is that they do not normally need to be laundered, be sure to make a note of fabric content and care when you buy them. Different types of rayon, for example, later can look and feel like silk, and silks can look like linen. If the bag will receive heavy use, select fabrics designed for easy care. If using specialty fabrics, consider spot treating with dry-cleaning fluid if they get soiled, or just make another bag!

cotton

Cotton fabrics come in a variety of colors, prints, weights, and textures. They are easily pieced, quilted, and embellished. If the bag will experience heavy use and will be washed periodically, then prewash fabrics before cutting.

silk

Silk fabrics offer a lustrous feel and sheen in many weights from sheer chiffon to slubby dupioni. Some silks can be washed by hand to eliminate shrinkage later, but most fare better being dry-cleaned.

linen

Linen fabrics have a loose weave and wrinkle easily unless fused with an interfacing or backed with batting and quilted. These fabrics can be prewashed, but they are best when dry-cleaned.

polyester and blends

This is probably the most versatile fabric for ease of care. These fabrics can be prewashed with minimal shrinkage.

rayon

Rayon fabric is versatile in texture, color, and sheen. It can have the drape and luster of silk and, although it can be laundered and pressed with care, it is best dry-cleaned.

tapestry

Tapestry is a textile with a loose weave but can be fused with interfacing to stabilize it. Dry-clean for best results.

velvet and velveteen

Both fabrics have a directional nap. When cutting pattern pieces, all the pieces must be cut facing in the same direction. Dry-clean for best results. When necessary, press the wrong side of the fabric.

faux fur

Faux fur also has a nap and all the pattern pieces must be cut facing the same direction. Spot clean for best results.

leather and suede

Leather and suede are, of course, made from animal skins. Both are usually professionally cleaned.

ultrasuede

Ultrasuede® is a non-woven product that looks and feels like suede, but it is washable. It is great for cutwork designs and to create fringe because it does not ravel.

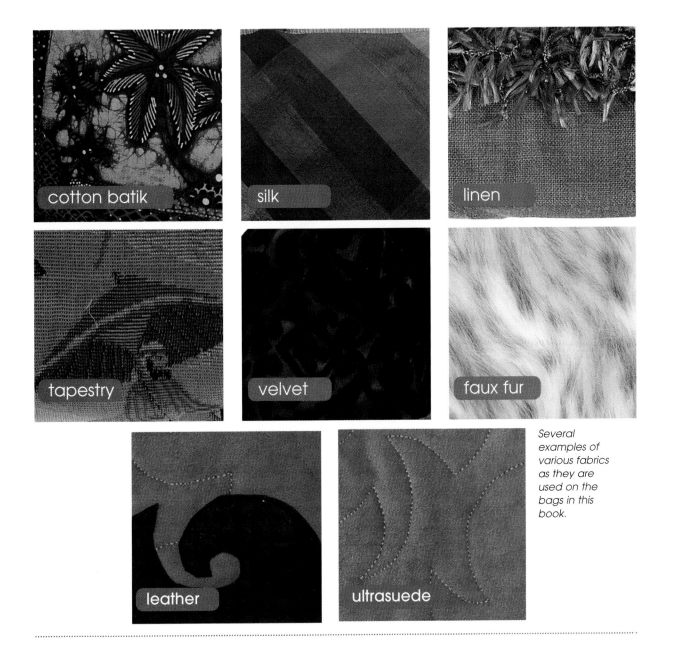

cotton batik

silk

linen

tapestry

velvet

faux fur

leather

ultrasuede

Several examples of various fabrics as they are used on the bags in this book.

stabilizers

● Batting is an important part of creating a great looking bag. Selecting the best product for a project is determined by the result you are trying to achieve. Incorporating cotton and silk batting will result in a very soft layer, polyester batting can result in a soft or firm layer (depending on the density and thickness), and using craft fleece will result in a firm layer.

Quilting requires sandwiching a top layer of fabric, a batting, and a bottom layer of fabric. ●

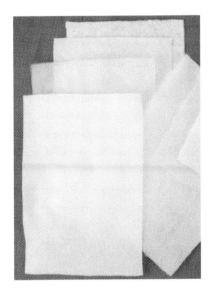

Batting, shown at right in various types, helps create lovely layers.

Battings, fleece, and interfacings are available with fusible finishes, which eliminates the need for spray adhesive and pins.

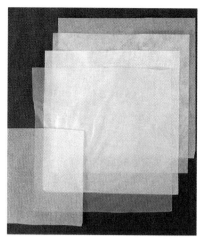

A variety of stabilizers.

cotton batting

When selecting cotton quilt batting, take several things—like the loft, density, color, and whether it has to be preshrunk—into consideration. Batting comes in a wide variety of thicknesses, which may be the main concern. First, decide how much loft you want in the quilted fabric. Most of the batting must be quilted approximately every two inches either by machine or hand. If left unquilted, the batting will migrate through daily use or washing and result in an uneven layer. The density may affect the ease of use for hand quilters. Batt color is the least important factor since its standard colors are cream and white, though black is available from some manufacturers. The batting color only matters when using white fabric.

An important consideration will be the amount of batt shrinkage to expect. If you want to achieve a vintage quilted look, then quilt the fabric and preshrink the entire quilted piece before cutting the purse pattern. Be sure to make this unit larger than the pattern, since quilting shrinks or pulls in the fabric sandwich—the more quilting the more shrinkage. If you would like a smooth, quilted layer, then the batting must be preshrunk before the sewing begins. Check the directions recommended by the manufacturer since they may vary.

silk batting

This luxurious batting can be pulled apart and placed in a layer that allows you to determine the loft and how much fabric to cover. It is available in pure white and does not need to be preshrunk. It also needs to be quilted every two to three inches and can be machine washed or dry-cleaned.

polyester batting

Polyester batting is available in a variety of lofts and densities, and does not have to be preshrunk. Quilting is optional with polyester batting, especially for small projects.

Polyester batting is now available sandwiched between two layers of sheer, non-woven polyester. This prevents migrating, bearding (when the batting comes through the fabric) even with dark fabrics, and eliminates the need for a layer of fabric underneath the batt when quilting. This batting is resistant to mildew and odors, and is nonflammable. I favor Simplicity Air-Lite® Bond Tight; I used it in many of the projects in this book. For any project in this book that calls for Air-Lite batting, however, you can substitute your choice of batting, but purchase the same amount of muslin and place it under your batting then treat the batting and muslin as one.

fleece

Needle-punched polyester fleece (prepared by punching with hundreds of needles to make it easier to sew through) is great for padding and quilting and creates a firm layer. The fleece is very dense and does not require a layer of fabric underneath when quilting.

fusible interfacing

Fusible nylon tricot interfacing is lightweight and very pliable. It even allows silk to keep a nice drape while adding a firmness that keeps the grain of the fabric straight and keeps the edges from raveling. It can be fused to knits, silks, and woven fabric, and is great for tapestry. It is available in black and white and can be preshrunk, although the shrinkage is very minimal. When pressing, use a Teflon® pressing sheet, and set the iron no higher than medium heat.

Fusible woven interfacing can be made of cotton, wool, polyester, nylon, rayon, or a blend. Woven interfacings are used with woven fabrics. A variety of products are available from sheer to heavy weights. Shrinkage is very minimal. A higher heat is permissible.

fusible web

Fusible web allows fabric to be fused to another fabric or to batting. The paper backing makes it easy to apply to the second surface. Lightweight fusible web is used for the projects in this book. Be aware that heavier weight fusibles sometimes show through lightweight fabrics such as dupioni silks.

spray adhesives

Spray adhesive works well on porous surfaces. Use it to temporarily adhere fabric to batting or fleece. Read the precautions on the product and spray in an isolated area with good ventilation.

Some essentials: spray adhesive, seam ripper, tape measure, marking pencil, and pin cushion.

needles

The appropriate needle is essential for sewing with different threads and fabrics. Lightweight fabrics typically use sizes 60 or 70, medium-weight fabrics use sizes 70 or 80, and heavyweight fabrics require sizes 80, 90, or 100. Realize that once fabrics are bonded with a batting, fleece, or interfacing, they become denser, so a larger needle size may be required. Needles that work well for heavier weights are denim, embroidery, quilting, and topstitch.

Specialty threads also require special needles. Metallic thread may require a Metalfil or topstitch needle, which has a deeper groove down the center to accommodate the specialty thread and helps to prevent fraying. Sewing a little slower and reducing the tension in your sewing machine may also help with fraying or breakage.

Test your needle with a variety of threads and fabrics. Keep a chart for future reference. A great reference for needles is *Point Well Taken* by Debbie Garbers and Janet O'Brien (In Cahoots, 1996).

threads

Polyester sewing thread is ideal for seams because of its tensile strength and wide variety of colors. This same thread can also be used for embellishing and quilting.

Rayon thread has a luster similar to silk and is excellent for embellishment techniques such as free-motion, satin stitching, and machine embroidery. Do not use rayon thread for seams because it does not have the strength for stress areas. Polyester embroidery thread has a lustrous sheen while keeping its strength. It is excellent for embellishment such as free-motion, satin stitching, and machine embroidery.

Metallic thread is available in several forms. Wrapped metallic thread is finer than regular sewing thread and conveys an elegant sheen. Flat metallic thread is like a ribbon and offers a bright shine.

For even more shine, use a holographic thread.

Variegated thread has several colors on the same strand. This creates a great effect with free-motion designs as well as when using the satin stitch technique. Variegated threads are available in rayon, polyester, embroidery, and metallic.

An assortment of threads, including polyester, rayon, metallic, holographic, and variegated varieties.

chapter 2

Sewing and Assembly Techniques

sewing techniques

free-motion

Free-motion, which is illustrated at the top of the page, can be one of the most creative methods of embellishment. It can be subtle, *and* it can be powerful. Use it to add dimension to your fabrics. Long, sweeping lines can soothe and short, angular lines can bring attention to an area. Use lines to draw and write names in script. It also has a utilitarian use of binding the layers of fabric and batting together while crafting a creative message.

Free-motion usually requires the ability to lower the feed dogs on the sewing machine and attach a darning or free-motion foot in place of the standard sewing foot. This allows the fabric to move freely between the foot and the throat plate. Some new free-motion feet work like walking feet, allowing you to leave the feed dogs up.

Stitch length is determined by the combination of how fast the needle is going up and down and how fast the sewer is moving the fabric. To move the fabric smoothly takes some practice and coordination. Practice by drawing some straight lines on quilting paper laid over a piece of fabric, and then practice stitching. Then, try a few curves, circles, and other various shapes.

Special adjustments to the machine are not needed unless using specialty threads. In that case, your needle selection and tension adjustments may have to be made to accommodate the thread.

satin stitching

Satin stitching, as illustrated in Figure 2-1, is a zigzag stitch sewn close together. It is used to create

Figure 2-1

buttonholes, but is capable of a lot more. The zigzag foot has a wide opening in the foot and a wide channel under the foot for the densely packed threads to escape.

Set the machine to a suitable zigzag width and shorten the stitch length. Most likely, there is a setting suitable for the satin stitch on the sewing machine. As you are stitching, practice moving the setting in small increments to see how close together the stitches need to be to cover the fabric completely.

Satin stitching can be used in various ways to add dimension, texture, and design to the fabric. It can be used to appliqué a motif as well as create a design with meandering lines. Covering a satin stitch with another layer can create a faux cord. Changing the width while sewing can create a feeling of movement within the line. Using different threads will also change the texture.

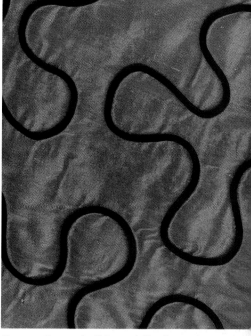

Free-motion embellishment, like the design shown here and on the facing page, adds dimension to any fabric.

topstitching

Topstitching, as shown in Figure 2-2 below, is a decorative stitch as well as a way of stabilizing an area. Regular sewing thread would make subtle stitching, while specialty threads and topstitching (heavier) threads really make a statement. The standard sewing foot is used with a slightly longer stitch length. Two rows of topstitching side by side, ⅜" apart, look like the double seams on jeans.

Figure 2-2

gathering stitch

The gathering stitch, illustrated in Figure 2-3, allows you to pull fabric together to create even, little folds. Here's how:

1. Use a standard sewing foot and set the machine to a longer stitch length—try number 4.

2. Sew a straight line, beginning and ending with a 4" length of thread.

3. Follow alongside the previous stitching with another line of stitching about ¼" apart.

4. Starting at one end, pull the threads from the same side of the fabric. Pull evenly and slowly until half the length is evenly gathered. Repeat, pulling the other thread tail.

5. Tie the ends.

Figure 2-3

stitch-in-the-ditch

This is a machine straight stitch, as shown in Figure 2-4, sewn directly into the seam line where two fabrics are joined together. The stitches are hidden when the threads match the color of the fabric and are virtually invisible. Frequently, a stitch-in-the-ditch serves two purposes, as it usually catches another fabric underneath and sews it in place.

Figure 2-4

basting

Basting, as in Figure 2-5 below, can be done on the sewing machine or by hand. The basting stitch on some sewing machines is just a very long, loose stitch; it's great for keeping large areas temporarily stable.

Basting by hand works well for keeping smaller areas or items in place temporarily with more precision. The threads are removed easily.

— — — — — — —

Figure 2-5

slipstitch

Slipstitch, for the purpose of this book, is best when done by hand. Shown in Figure 2-6, the slipstitch brings together two fabrics with a minimal amount of thread showing. Here's how:

1. Take needle carefully into the fabric a short distance then into the other fabric a short distance forward.

2. Continue to repeat the process.

3. Bury the knot in between the fabrics.

backstitch by hand

The backstitch is similar to the basting stitch, but because you make shorter stitch lengths, it is more secure. Backstitching creates a short stitch on the surface and a long stitch on the underside. This stitch is used for the projects in the book to attach the beaded fringe to the fabric. Referring to Figure 2-7, here's how:

1. Take a forward stitch (1) and pull the thread through.

2. Return the needle back into the hole of the prior stitch (2) and angle the needle forward to the original direction for the next stitch (3).

3. Continue on as in steps 1 and 2 (4-7).

4. Knot at the end.

Slip stitch by hand

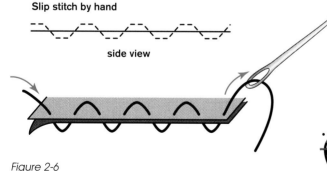

side view

Figure 2-6

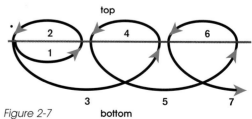

Figure 2-7

assembly techniques

fabric layout and cutting

Most of the projects have patterns, but a few are just squares or rectangles produced by measurements. Make paper patterns using these dimensions. Place the patterns on the fabric's straight-of-grain (which runs parallel to the selvage) unless otherwise noted. Be sure to place the patterns to capture the fabric's design motifs. Fold the fabric with wrong sides together when cutting two identical pattern pieces to assure a front and back. Be sure to include notches and clip marks.

Use very sharp scissors to guarantee accuracy. Kai brand scissors are made with micro-serrated teeth to reduce slippage on even the sheerest fabric.

Strips won't require patterns if you use a rotary cutter, mat, and ruler. Learn to use these tools properly and safely. Be aware that a rotary cutter blade is a razor-in-the-round and, if handled improperly, can send careless sewers to the emergency room.

The bias of the fabric is found by folding the fabric at a 90-degree angle from the grain line. Patterns cut this way will stretch in width and height. Strips cut on the bias will have the ability to stretch a little, and tubes made on the bias will have a nicer form.

sewing, pressing, and trimming a seam

A standard seam has a stitch length of 10 to 12 stitches per inch. The stitch length should vary depending on the thickness and weave of the fabric. Always backstitch a few stitches when beginning and ending a seam to lock the stitch and prevent seams from coming open, especially when turning bags inside out.

A seam should be pressed once to set the stitching into the weave of the fabric, and then pressed open. This makes it easier to press the seam open smoothly.

Be sure to use a pressing cloth if using steam. If steam is not required, a Teflon pressing sheet is great for protecting specialty fabrics. It also protects the iron from any fusible residue. The mini iron is handy for getting into small places as well as for pressing seams.

When trimming seams, take into consideration the weave of the fabric. If the fabric has a loose

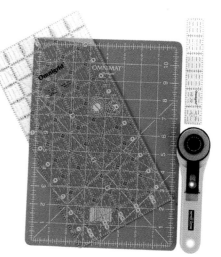

Measuring and cutting essentials: rotary cutter, mat, and rulers.

weave, it may be best not to trim, or trim only very little away. Cottons and fabrics with a more substantial weave can be trimmed to ¼" seam allowances. Seam edges can also be finished with serging, a zigzag stitch, by sewing another line of stitching right next to the previous stitching, or with pinking shears.

Batting should be trimmed to reduce bulk. Trim the batt right down to the seam.

If batting or fleece is fused to the fashion fabric, you may cut away the seam allowances before sewing seams to reduce bulk, or consider grading (layering) the seams. If batting or fleece is not fused, then it should be quilted together or leave the seam allowances and trim away after the seams are sewn. This will secure the batting or fleece.

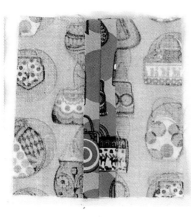

Referring to the progression of photos above: 1) Sew the seam and press. 2) Press the seam open. 3) Trim the batting from the seam.

creating tubes for loops and straps

Tubes are created by folding strips of fabric in half lengthwise and then sewing a seam along one long edge.

Tubes cut on the grain of the fabric, as shown in Figure 2-8, do not stretch, which is great for creating loops for handles that will bear some weight. Figure 2-9 shows how a tube that is cut on the grain is stitched.

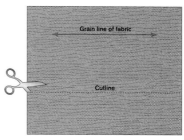

Figure 2-8

Tube on the grain

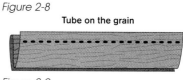

Figure 2-9

Tubes created from bias strips stretch a little and should be pulled taut when sewing the seam to avoid breakage later. Tubes cut on the bias also take on the shape of what is placed inside, such as cording for a round strap or boning for a stiff, flat strap. When a very narrow tube is needed, a bias tube is easier to turn right-side out. Here's how to cut the fabric to create a bias strip:

1. Fold one corner of a rectangular piece of fabric over and cut away the diagonal fold, as shown in Figure 2-10.

2. Cut a diagonal line, as in Figure 2-11, about 3" in from the edge you cut in step 1.

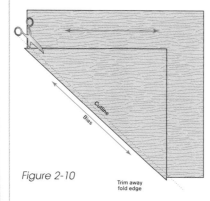

Figure 2-10

Trim away fold edge

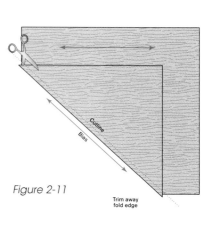

Figure 2-11

Trim away fold edge

3. Cut away the right angles at each end of the bias strip, as in Figure 2-12, to create a rectangle.

4. Fold strip with wrong sides together, pin, and stitch with ¾" seam allowance. Turn right-side out, as in Figure 2-13.

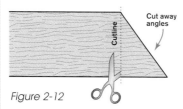

Cut away angles

Figure 2-12

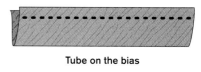

Tube on the bias

Figure 2-13

Trim the seams if the tubes will be filled. If the tubes will not be filled, leave the seam allowance to help give the tube additional body.

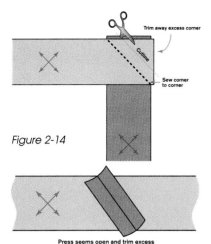

Figure 2-14

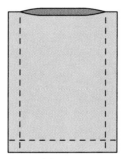

Press seems open and trim excess

Figure 2-15

Figures 2-14 and 2-15 at the left show ways to connect strips that were cut in Figure 2-11 to create longer bias strips when needed.

All fabric tubes can be turned right-side out with a Fasturn (available in several width sizes). A fabric tube is placed over the outside of a metal Fasturn tube and a long, straight wire is sent through the metal tube to catch a bit of the fabric at the other end. The fabric tube is then pulled through the inside of the metal tube, and is reversed right-side out as it exits the metal tube. Another option is to add a cord while pulling it through. The Fasturn fills the tube with the cord while turning it right-side out.

For short loops, make a long tube, turn it right-side-out, and then cut it in smaller increments. Use these to attach the specialty handle hardware. Stitch narrow tubes to pockets to clip on key chains or tassels. Make longer tubes for straps. Fill them with cord for a firm strap. Leave unfilled for a soft handle. Consider topstitching down each long edge for detail.

creating a square, flat bag bottom

Squaring off the corners of the bag is a simple method for creating a flat bottom for the bag.

1. Sew the side seams and the bottom seam of the bag, as in Figure 2-16, trim, and press all the seams.

2. Fold the bottom corner of the bag by aligning the bottom seam with the side seam with right sides together. This creates a triangle.

3. Referring to Figure 2-17, measure down the seam that is in the center of the triangle. Make a mark and draw a horizontal line perpendicular to that center seam. Sew across that line.

4. Repeat steps 2 and 3 for the other side. The farther you measure down that center seam, the wider the seam will be.

5. Face the points of the triangle toward the center and tack in place, as in Figure 2-18.

6. Place a piece of plastic canvas grid (available at hobby, craft, and stitchery stores) cut to size to add stability to the bottom of the bag.

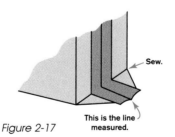

Figure 2-16

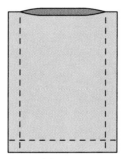

Sew.

This is the line measured.

Figure 2-17

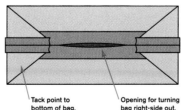

Tack point to bottom of bag.

Opening for turning bag right-side out.

Figure 2-18

adding metal feet to the bottom of the bag

Metal feet can be added to the bottom of the bag after creating the flat area.

1. Place the feet on the bag by measuring in ¾" from each side of a corner, as shown in Figure 2-19, and make a mark. Repeat for the remaining three corners.

Bottom of bag

Figure 2-19

2. Using very sharp scissors, clip a small slit to match the width of the prongs of the metal feet.

3. Hold the metal foot and push the prongs through the slit, as shown in Figure 2-20.

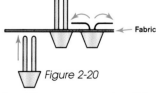

Fabric

Figure 2-20

4. Bend the prongs apart until they are horizontal, as in Figure 2-21. This will keep them in place. For a sturdier surface, push the prongs through the plastic canvas.

Plastic canvas

Fabric

chapter 3

Embellishments, Closures, and Specialty Handles

embellishments

● From tassels and fringe to buttons, charms, and beads, embellishments allow you to add those impressive little elements that define your personal style.●

tassels

Tassels add instant magic to your bags. They can be found in almost every color and size. Purchase them in fabric stores, craft sections, and home decorating departments. Attach them to handles or loops, dangle them from the bottom of bags, create pins, and group them together for a more dramatic look. They add style with so little effort.

Rayon tassels help to add excitement to your design.

On Travel Tokyo, pages 124-126, notice how just adding a single tassel to the front creates an air of elegance.

fringe

Bead, feather, and fiber fringes are all the rage. They are just the right touch for a one-of-a-kind bag. The items are purchased already attached to cotton tape, which makes them easy to add to your project. They are sold as yardage or come in prepackaged segments. Some fringes are easy to machine sew on the bag and others may require sewing by hand.

Dimensional fringe.

Beaded fringes are available in many colors, fringe lengths, and bead types. Glass, plastic, and metallic beads are popular.

Feather fringe is exquisite and creates immediate drama. Natural and dyed feathers can be found in many colors, lengths, and mixtures. When using feathers, keep the rest of the design uncomplicated ... the feathers say plenty.

Create a simple bag as the base and cover it with feather fringe for a fast, yet elegant, project.

Fiber fringe comes in all shapes and forms—fluffy, flat, tasseled, sprinkled with glitter, studded with metallic beads, braids, cords, knitted—so there is something for everyone.

With beading all the rage, embellish your purse with some of the many breathtaking baubles now available and end up with stunning results like those on the fringe of Black Tie and Tails, at left and on pages 37-39.

Fiber fringe embellishes the For the Love of Lavender bag, shown above here and again fully detailed on pages 46-49.

The Rue des Francs-Bourgeois, shown here above and with full instructions on pages 64-67, has a beautiful feather fringe at the top.

Feather fringes are available in different lengths, colors, and type of feather.

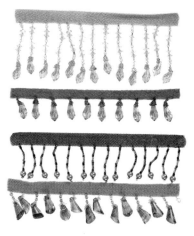

Beaded fringe, in various colors and lengths, adds motion.

buttons

Buttons are now no longer just for buttonholes. Used as embellishments, they can adorn any place on a bag or, strung with a tassel, become an even more interesting point of focus, or made into a pin like the one that decorates the Sedona Satchel, pages 40-42. Use vintage buttons found at antique fairs, raku clay buttons created by artists, carved wood buttons from craft fairs, covered buttons, or metal buttons from old uniforms.

charms, asian coins, and shaped stone pendants

Charms, coins, and pendants with a hole or loop can be used to embellish. Cords, braids, tassels, or a snap hook will attach them to your bag. Sometimes one is the perfect touch to personalize an otherwise basic bag—or add several.

A rich, artful button can be the single ornament that lifts all the components to the same high level of quality, as with the Sedona Sunset purse shown at right and with full instructions on pages 40-42.

An interesting Asian fan charm adds that hint of personalization to the Shades of Monet bag, which is detailed on pages 78-80.

hand-sewn beads

A few beads sewn on by hand can enhance a fabric or quilted design. Use beads one at a time or in strands. A carefully placed sprinkling of beads in the same color as the fabric adds an elegant, subtle look while beads grouped together in vibrant colors to create a flower can make a great impact.

If the surface will experience a lot of contact, add single beads one at a time and tie them off in the back to secure, as shown in Figure 3-1.

If contact is not a concern, individual beads can be sewn through twice and then the needle could move on to another bead until a few have been sewn and knotted, as shown in Figure 3-2.

For strands of beads, use a couching technique. A strand of beads is positioned and a separate needle and thread sews the beads in place by stitching over the thread that holds the beads together.

Beads sewn and tied off.

Figure 3-1

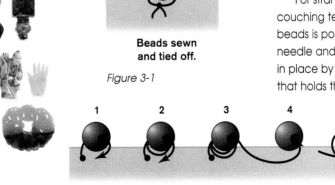

| 1 | 2 | 3 | 4 | 5 | 6 |

Sew the bead twice.   *Figure 3-2*   **Go through twice.**   **Move on to next bead.**

stencils, fabric ink pad, and metallic fabric paint

Printing with stencils is a great way to design your own fabric. It allows you to add a motif specific in size, color, design, and location. Add one motif or create a repeat design. Stencils can be found in thousands of shapes, usually cut from Mylar®. Now, die-cut stencils are available with a sticky backing, which allows you to change your mind and move it around until you are pleased. The sticky backing also allows you to move your project to a safe place to dry without disturbing the wet design.

Fabric inkpads and metallic fabric paints offer different results.

The fabric inkpad is used with a sponge-topped dauber that is pressed on the inkpad and picks up the ink. It is then pressed to the fabric through the stencil with a tapping motion, thereby transferring the ink. The fabric inks bond with the fabric and are heat-set with an iron. When the paint is dry there is no change in the texture of the fabric. Metallic fabric paints lay on top of the fabric and create a smooth texture on the fabric's surface. These paints are applied with paintbrushes and are set with heat. Both methods offer immediate gratification.

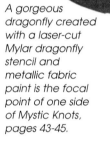

A gorgeous dragonfly created with a laser-cut Mylar dragonfly stencil and metallic fabric paint is the focal point of one side of Mystic Knots, pages 43-45.

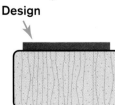

The back side stencil on the Mystic Knots bag.

Stencil Method

1. Place the stencil on the fabric, as shown in Figure 3-3.

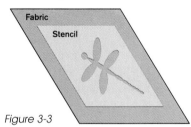

Figure 3-3

2. Use either a brush to paint in the fabric paint thickly or a dauber filled with fabric ink to pounce lightly on the stenciled area, as shown.

Figure 3-4

3. When finished, just peel away the stencil and reuse.

Rubber Stamp Method

Another option is to use a rubber stamp, rather than a stencil, in concert with the fabric inkpad.

1. Hold the rubber stamp upside-down, as shown in Figure 3-5.

Figure 3-5

2. Pounce the rubber stamp with the fabric ink pad, as shown in Figure 3-6.
3. Stamp design onto the fabric and let dry.

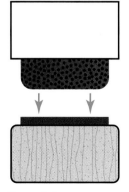

Figure 3-6

closures

A closure is not necessary with every bag, but if you plan to carry anything valuable inside, you will probably appreciate the extra security closures bring with them.

These two bags show just two options for flaps. The projects, Weekend in Acapulco (above left) and Heavy Date (above), are detailed on pages 88-90 and 84-87, respectively.

flaps

Flaps are a decorative way to help keep a bag closed and can be added to almost any project by placing them in the top seam of the bag. Try creating your own flaps in any shape or size. A flap can span the width of the bag or fit between the handles. Figure 3-7 shows several flap styles.

Add a loop closure, Velcro®, or a magnetic snap to secure a flap either on the outside or inside the bag, as shown in Figure 3-8.

To encourage the flap to lay flat, weight it down with beaded fringe, as in the Heavy Date piece shown in the photo above.

Experiment with flaps as a source of embellishment and to add a little security for treasures inside, as in Figure 3-9.

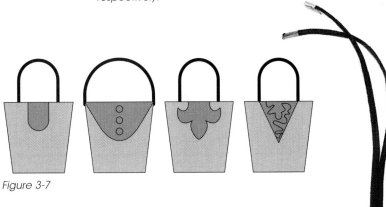

Figure 3-7

Figure 3-8

Figure 3-9

An assortment of embellishments, from left, that can be used specifically for closures: braid, coin, and tassel, gold knots, dragonfly ornaments, purse feet, and Chinese frog closure.

magnetic snaps

Magnetic snaps are a quick and easy way to add a closure to your bag. They stay locked together because of the magnetic attraction. Each magnet is held within a decorative metal ring that is backed with two prongs. Here's how to use them:

1. Cut two small slits in the desired location, as shown in Figure 3-10. Make sure the area is stabilized with batting or add a small piece of interfacing to reinforce the location.

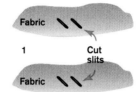

Figure 3-10

3. Once the prongs are pushed through, pull them apart and press down flat onto the fabric, locking the magnet in place, as in Figure 3-12.

2. Push the prongs through the slits in the fabric, as shown.

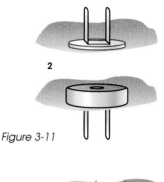

Figure 3-11

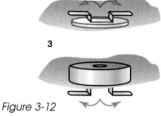

Figure 3-12

Magnetic snaps, like the one used on the Zanzibar, shown above and detailed on pages 105-108, add a professional finish and security to purses.

loops and braid loops

Loops can be created from the same fabric as the bag's construction or from braids. Here's how:

For braided loops:

1. Measure the button or toggle and add enough length to the loop so the fastener will slip through, but not so loose that it will pull out. Be sure to add seam allowances to each end to sew the loop into the seam of the bag.

2. If using a purchased braid, cut it to the desired length, but not before wrapping the ends with transparent tape prior to cutting to help prevent unraveling.

3. Once cut, achieve a dramatic look by adding tassels or coins to the loop, as shown in the examples in Figures 3-13, 3-14, and 3-15.

4. Sew braided loop into the bag's seam.

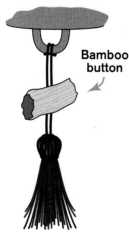

Bamboo button

Figure 3-13

Figure 3-14

Figure 3-15

For fabric tube loops:

1. Fold a strip of fabric in half lengthwise with wrong sides together.

2. Sew open raw edge shut.

3. Turn right-side out with a Fasturn and cut to the desired length.

4. Embellish, if desired with tassels or coins, just as with the braided loop.

5. Sew into place on the bag.

drawstring closures

Various drawstring techniques are used and adequately detailed in the instructions of those purses affected: Black Tie and Tails, pages 37-39; Sedona Sunset, pages 40-42; Mystic Knot, pages 43-45; and Rodeo Drive, pages 50-53.

specialty zippers

The use of zippers has been kept to a minimum is this book, as only one project, Shibori Purse on pages 95-97, contains a zipper closure. The directions for that purse are somewhat unique to that type of purse alone and are therefore detailed within the project instructions.

A braided loop-and-tassel closure, such as the one on the Cochin Clutch detailed on pages 98-101, adds a functional yet fun finishing touch to a bag.

Specialty zippers.

Use a zipper closure, like that on the Shibori Purse shown here and with complete instructions on pages 95-97, for optimal security.

specialty handles

A handle can set the tone for the bag. Mix up the textures: Combine shiny faux lacquer with soft Ultrasuede, bamboo beautifully carved by nature with tapestry fabrics, and smooth faux marble with printed chenille. Let your imagination run wild and use two acrylic bracelets with a lace bag!

bamboo/rattan, wood, and faux materials

There is an incredible array of handles available made of bamboo, wood, faux marble, and faux lacquer. Most are shaped in the traditional upside-down "U," but some are circular, and some have curled ends.

Some of the handles come with hardware that has a removable screw, which allows you to make the bag and add the handles at the end. And all handles can be added with fabric or braid ties.

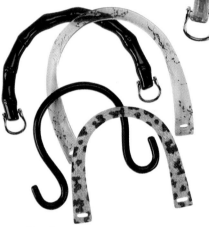

Handles come in quite a large selection of colors, textures, and materials.

A twisted rattan handle, secured to the bag with tied braid loops, adds the perfect finish to the Safari Satchel, which is detailed on pages 54-56.

The Obi Orange Blossom bag, with full instructions on pages 115-117, has handles that came with the hardware to attach them.

Here's how to attach a handle with hardware:

1. Referring to Figure 3-16, place the U-shaped metal connector piece through a fabric loop.
2. Match the holes on the U-shaped connector piece to those at the end of one handle side.
3. Insert screw through holes.

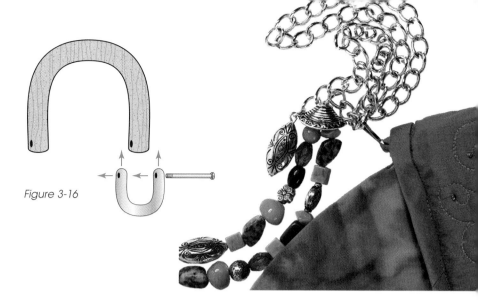

Figure 3-16

belts

A beaded belt makes a stunning handle. Here's how:

1. Find a belt with a snap hook at one end and a chain at the other end.
2. Make a purse with a fabric loop at each side of the bag. (The bag can be used as a clutch bag when the loops are tucked inside the bag.)
3. Snap the hook into one of the loops, place a purchased snap hook on the other loop, and snap onto the chain portion of the belt.

Select a belt with a snap hook/lanyard at one end and a chain at the other end for a remarkable handle, like the one used on the Weekend in Acapulco project, pages 88-90.

polyester stays and plastic hose

Use items that are not normally used as handles.

Polyester stay (or boning) is used in garment construction to keep an area (like the bodice) stiff. Use them to fill fabric tube handles that will keep their shape.

Plastic hose can also be used for handles that maintain their shape while creating a round handle.

Here's how:

1A. Create a leather tube, as instructed on page 113, that is slightly longer than the hose handle piece. When using leather, leave the seam on the outside because the leather may be too hard to turn inside-out. Trim the seam allowance close to the seam and tuck on the inside curve. This technique is used in this book only in the construction of St. Moritz, pages 112-114.

1B. Create a fabric tube that is turned right-side out and fill it with the polyester stay. This is the technique used in the Shibori Purse instructions, pages 95-97.
2. Attach the handle to the bag.

The Starlet project, shown at right and with its full instructions on pages 91-94, incorporates polyester stay inside the bag opening to keep its shape.

chapter 4

Projects

what's your style?

The following projects are divided by bag styles, with each of those styles detailed below. Match the helpful icon below to that on the project instruction pages, and you'll know what style you're about to bring to life.

flat totes

The flat tote bag is probably the easiest and quickest purse to make, until you begin embellishing—then it can be as complicated as you like! This flat bag easily rolls up in your suitcase, ready to spring into action at a moment's notice. A pleasing shape for this bag is the vertical rectangle, although it works fine as a square, triangle, or circle. The great part is that it requires very few steps, really: You take one shape, cut out four pieces of fabric, and select some kind of handle. If you have a great fabric in mind, and just need a quick tote bag, you're ready to go. But sometimes, you've purchased that perfect little piece of handmade batik, a cute little scarf at the fair (that will not fit around your neck, no way), or you were in a workshop and made an embellished sample of fabric. You've put your treasure away, brought it back out, pinned it to the wall, and no one can appreciate it but you. So use it as the focal point and frame it with a fabric that enhances it—remember how a frame and matting can make all the difference for a work of art. For the lining, use the same fabric or select a coordinating fabric if using one of the two fabrics to create handles. If you are using specialty handles then the fabrics do not have to coordinate. Then comes the fun part: adding pockets, appliqué, quilting, and jewelry.

drawstring pouches

Drawstring pouches are so versatile … and hold more than they look like they might hold. Since you're working with drawstring closures, some sewers may find them easier to make. The bags in this section all come from one basic pattern, but feel free to alter and design to suit your tastes. The basic pattern accommodates beads, fringes, feathers, buttons and anything else you may fancy!

the a- and v-shaped bags

The A- and V-shaped bags can be made of just one fabric or as shown with two different fabrics. Just turning the pattern upside-down makes the two different bag shapes. That simple turn creates a dramatic difference. The embellishment and the choice of handles also create a different look each time. This bag can be reversible by selecting wonderful fabrics for both sides.

large totes with round handles

Everyone needs a tote this size to take everything along: cell phone, wallet, fabric swatches, shopping list, pens, keys, and a paperback to read while waiting for an appointment. How nice to have everything traveling in style!

small shoulder bags and hip bags with flaps

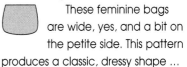

These versatile bags are quick to make and can be worn as shoulder bags or hip bags. Just make the straps long enough to hang from your shoulder or tie around your waist. Strip-piecing and quilting the body of the bag with your favorite fabrics will give these bags plenty of personality.

wide bags

These feminine bags are wide, yes, and a bit on the petite side. This pattern produces a classic, dressy shape … perfect for a special evening or event, and they're fun to embellish with feathers, beads, jewelry, and unique fabrics. Try one!

large pieced totes

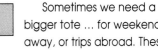

Sometimes we need a bigger tote … for weekends away, or trips abroad. These bags are so simple to make, embellish, and take-along. You'll be surprised how quickly you can put one together!

World
Traveler

I created this tote bag with a Japanese furoshiki. Long ago, the furoshiki was similar to a bath mat at the public bathhouses; wet clothes were wrapped in this "towel" and carried home. Today, the furoshiki has evolved into beautifully designed squares of fabric for gift-wrapping or is used as a decorative wall hanging. In this case, the size of the furoshiki dictated the size of the tote bag. The furoshiki with the geisha is a 17" square. The one used for the back is slightly larger so the remainder of the fabric is used to create the handles. The tote bag and handles are lined with black cotton fabric and the top edge is finished with a black bias trim. In place of a furoshiki, use fabric yardage.

finished size
16½" x 16"

fabric and notions

½-yard fabric,
or 17" square Geisha furoshiki

½-yard floral fabric or floral furoshiki

½-yard Air-Lite batting*

½-yard black cotton lining

3" x 33" black cotton bias strip

Adhesive spray

Sewing thread to match

Decorative rayon
or poly embroidery thread

Straight pins

Scissors

Straight stitch sewing machine foot

Free-motion sewing machine foot

Quilting needle

Fasturn

Measuring tape

Iron

*For any project in this book that calls for Air-Lite batting; you can substitute your choice of batting, but purchase the same amount of muslin and place it under your batting; treat the batting and muslin as one.

note

In place of the black cotton lining for the inside of the bag, use another print so it can be reversible. Switch colors for the handle lining and bias trim so it will match the inside and the outside.

prepare

1. Cut, as follows:
   - 17" Geisha furoshiki square
   - 17" floral furoshiki square
   - two 2½" x 18" floral furoshiki pieces
   - two 17" batting squares
   - two 2½" x 18" batting pieces
   - two 17" black cotton lining squares
   - two 2½" x 18" black cotton lining pieces

embellish

1. Using a straight stitch foot, a decorative thread, and a quilting or Metalfil needle, sew along some of the interesting straight lines of the geisha furoshiki, as shown in Figure 4-1.

2. Spray the wrong side of the Geisha furoshiki square and place over the batting. Hand-press to smooth.
3. Pin in several places.
4. Repeat for the floral furoshiki square that is placed on the other side of the bag.

2. Change to the free-motion foot to follow curved lines. Quilting the floral furoshiki also requires the free-motion foot and decorative thread.
3. Echo quilt or meander around the flowers in the fabric.

(continued)

Right side of fabric

Figure 4-1

assemble

1. Place the quilted geisha and floral furoshiki with right sides together and sew the sides and bottom with a ½" seam with regular sewing thread. Press seams toward the floral furoshiki. Set aside.

2. Place each set of the black lining pieces with right sides together and sew the sides and the bottom with a ½" seam allowance.

3. Press seams in the opposite direction of the furoshiki.

straps

1. Place one strip of floral furoshiki with one strip of black fabric with right sides together. Place one strip of batting under the black fabric. Sew the long sides with a ½" seam allowance, as shown in Figure 4-2. Do the same for the other strap.

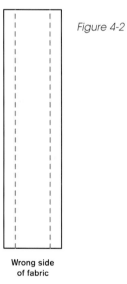

Figure 4-2

**Wrong side
of fabric**

The exquisite detail of the bag's center motif.

2. Turn the straps right-side out. A Fasturn helps to reverse the straps. Press flat with seams at the side.

3. Crease the center front and back at the top of the quilted furoshiki bag and pin mark as a starting place for the strap locations.

4. Place each end of a strap 2" out from the center location on the front of the bag. Pin. Sew ½" from the edge. Do the same for the strap placed on the back.

trim

1. With right sides together, sew the short ends of the black bias with a ½" seam allowance. Trim to ¼". Press the seam open.

2. Fold the bias in half lengthwise with wrong sides together and press. Pin the bias around the top edge of the bag against the quilted furoshiki. Align the bias seam with the bag's seam. The raw edge of the bias should align with the raw edges at the top of the bag.

3. Sew a ½" seam from the raw edge. Turn the bias so the folded edge is facing up, and press.

4. Fold the edge over so it meets the stitching line on the inside of the bag and pin the bias in place. Stitch-in-the-ditch between the bag and the bias, making sure it catches the folded edge of the bias on the inside, or hand sew in place. Press.

Bengal Batik

I bought this small piece of batik at a quilt festival because of its beautiful design and colors dyed by hand. It cried out for framing, which meant the tote bag had to be larger than my piece of batik. Because this traditional batik was created on cotton, I selected two coordinating batik cotton fabrics. The lining is also cotton batik yardage. Pockets always come in handy with these totes, so the batik panel was used to create one. Bamboo handles, just the right color, are used in place of fabric handles, and a coordinating lining makes it reversible. The same lining for the bag is used to line the pocket. To frame a batik, follow this simple method: Determine the finished size, measure the center batik piece, and add a enough inches on all sides to reach your desired measurements, plus ½" seam allowances.

finished size
16" x 13½"

fabric and notions

11½" x 11" handpainted batik panel

½-yard yellow batik print

½-yard brown batik print

¾-yard Air-Lite batting

2 5½" bamboo handles

Sewing thread to match

Adhesive spray

Decorative brown rayon 30- or 40-weight or poly embroidery thread

Velcro (optional)

Pins

Scissors

Iron

Measuring tape

Charm

prepare

1. Cut, as follows:
   - 11½" x 11" handpainted batik panel
   - 11½" x 11" yellow batik print piece
   - 6" x 12" yellow batik print piece
   - 3" x 11" yellow batik print strip (made in step 4 of pocket detail)
   - 2" x 3" yellow batik print piece
   - two 17" x 15" yellow batik print pieces
   - two 17" x 15" brown batik print pieces
   - 2" x 12" brown batik print strip
   - two 17" x 15" batting pieces
   - 11½" x 11" batting piece

2. Spray adhesive on the wrong side of the batik panel and place on batting. Pin in several places.

3. Spray adhesive on the wrong side of the two pieces of brown batik. Place the wrong side on batting. Pin around each piece in several places.

4. Using a decorative thread that either coordinates or contrasts, use free-motion to outline parts of the design on the batik panel. In this case, the horizon of the landscape and a few trees were outlined.

5. Use free-motion to quilt the other two larger pieces.

6. Press all pieces lightly.

joining the pocket

1. Place the quilted batik panel and the yellow batik print lining with right sides together.

2. Sew around the perimeter, leaving a 4" opening at the bottom, as shown in Figure 4-3. Backstitch at beginning and end.

Right side of fabric

Figure 4-3

3. Turn it right-side out, tuck the seam allowances inside at the bottom opening, and press lightly. Place some Velcro under the sun design on the lining fabric. Use free-motion to quilt around the sun as well as to sew the Velcro in place.

4. Center the batik on the right side of one of the larger quilted pieces, measure, and adjust the sides so they are of equal distance from the edges.

5. Next, measure the distance at the top and bottom and shift the batik toward the top so that the distance at the bottom is greater by ½" to 1".

6. Pin in place and sew around the sides and bottom of the batik pocket, reinforcing at the beginning and end.

7. Stitch the other side of the Velcro to the bag.

The Asian coin charm and burnt bamboo handles are great functional accessories.

optional small pocket detail

1. Fold the width of the fashion fabric lining pocket piece in half with right sides together.

2. Create a 1½"-wide pleat by sewing along the dotted lines provided. Be sure to backstitch when ending.

3. Press open, aligning the center of the pleat, as shown in Figure 4-4. Fold the strip with right sides together lengthwise, press, and cut in half.

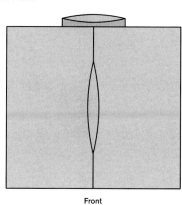

Front

Figure 4-4

4. This strip is made into a doubled binding similar to applying a double-fold binding to a quilt. Fold the strip in half to 1½" x 11". Referring to Figure 4-5, apply its edges along the batik fabric edge and stitch in place with a ½" seam. Roll the binding over to encase the raw edges and stitch down. There is now a doubled finished ½" binding on both sides of the fashion fabric. Cut away excess fabric.

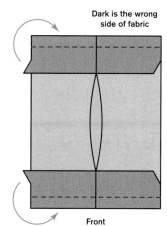

Dark is the wrong side of fabric

Front

Figure 4-5

5. Press open, place over the seam, and allow the folded edge to meet the stitching, as shown in Figure 4-6. Pin in place from the front.

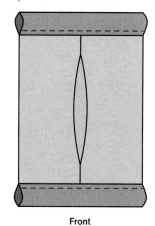

Front

Figure 4-6

6. Topstitch close to the edge of the seam on the strip and then topstitch close to the edge of the fold, as in Figure 4-7. Do the same

(continued)

for the bottom of the pocket, but eliminate the last seam close to the edge of the fold.

Light stitching lines are the previous stitch

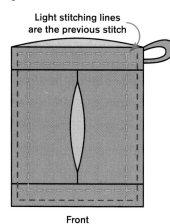

Front

Figure 4-7

7. For the small loop: With right sides together, fold the small square in half, and sew with a ½" seam allowance. Turn right-side out and press. Fold it in half and tuck it under the side of the pocket edge near the top, as in Figure 4-8, and pin.

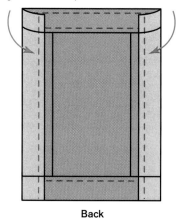

Back

Figure 4-8

8. Fold the ½" seam allowances of the sides under and press. Sew a line of stitching along the sides ½" in from the edge.

9. Position the wrong side of the pocket against the right side of the fashion fabric lining anywhere you choose. In this case, it was positioned at the center (width) and 2½" from the top edge of the yellow batik lining. Pin in place and topstitch close to the folded edge of the pocket along the sides and bottom. Make sure to catch that little loop in the stitching.

Change your spots, so to speak, by bringing the inside of this bag out.

loops

1. With right sides together, fold the 2" x 12" strip of fabric in half lengthwise.

2. Guide the folded edge along the ⅝" marking on your sewing machine throat plate and sew the entire length. Turn the loop right-side out with the Fasturn.

3. Cut the strip into four 3" pieces. Fold each piece in half.

handles

1. Measure the distance between the handle hardware and divide that measurement in half.

2. Now, fold the top of the quilted brown batik front and back pieces in half and mark each center with a pin.

3. Finally, measure out from the center pin in both directions and re-mark with the handle's half-measurement.

4. Position each folded loop along these handle marks, making sure the raw edge of the loop aligns with the raw edge of the quilted brown batik pieces. Pin and sew in place.

assemble

1. Place the quilted brown batik pieces with right sides together. Sew the sides and bottom with a ½" seam allowance. Trim the excess batting from the seams. Press the seams toward the back of the bag. Turn right-side out.

2. Place the yellow batik lining with right sides together. Sew the sides and the bottom, leaving a 5" opening (reinforce at beginning and end). Press the seams toward the front of the bag.

3. Place the quilted brown batik bag inside the yellow batik lining bag with right sides together. Sew around the top with a ½" seam allowance, making sure to catch the four loops. Turn the bag right-side out through the 5" opening. Tuck the seam allowance inside the opening and slipstitch by hand to close. Lightly press the entire bag.

Black Tie
and Tails

This drawstring pouch is made using Devoré (burn-out) velvet. This interesting fabric has a velvet pile design surrounded by sheer chiffon. It is easy to work with and requires only a little hand basting to prevent the fabric from shifting during sewing. The bag is lined with silk dupioni in a light color to show through the sheer portion of the Devoré velvet. A rayon braid is used for the drawstrings for ease of pulling through the casing and a strip of beaded fringe is added to just the bottom of the bag.

finished size

10½" x 8"*

*Size does not account for fringe length.

fabric and notions

½-yard Devoré velvet

½-yard silk dupioni

2 34"-long braided cords

Ballpoint sewing machine needle

10" beaded fringe

Threads to match each fabric

Safety pin

Pins

Scissors

Patterns

---

note

Now is a chance to use your vintage hankies and small pieces of special fabrics.

Use less or more beaded fringe, depending on what you can find and your personal preference. Each bag's finished appearance will be different depending on your selections. The beaded fringe I found is sometimes used around a dress neckline so it was a unique shape, but a perfect fit for the bag since the pattern's shape is a "V."

prepare

1. Cut, as follows:
- two velvet pieces of pattern #ONE-1 (body)
- two silk dupioni pieces of pattern #ONE-1 (body)
- two velvet pieces of pattern #ONE-2 (casing)

embellish

1. Place the strip of beading along the stay-stitched edge at the bottom of a velvet body piece. Make sure the fringe is facing the center of the bag and that the tape is toward the fabric's raw edge, as shown in Figure 4-9.

2. Bring the beginning of the beaded fringe to the stay-stitched line.

3. Pin in place then baste in place by hand. Make sure that the stitching does not pull and gather stitches. It must lay flat, as shown in the accompanying photo below.

2. Stay-stitch ½" from the edge across the top of both velvet body pieces.

3. Stay-stitch ½" from the edge along the bottom center of one of the velvet body pieces (about 10").

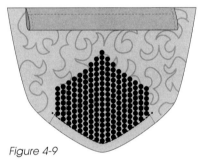

Figure 4-9

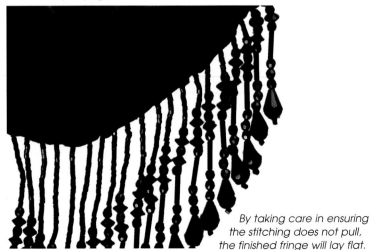

By taking care in ensuring the stitching does not pull, the finished fringe will lay flat.

casing

1. Finish the short ends of the Devoré velvet strips by folding the raw edges of the velvet over ¼" to the wrong side and then folding it again using a total of ½", as in Figure 4-10. Pin. Machine-stitch close to the folded edge.

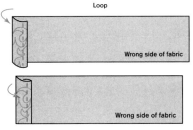

Figure 4-10

assemble

1. Place the velvet body pieces with right sides together and pin around the perimeter. Make sure the beads and the loop are on the inside, sandwiched between the two fabrics.

2. Sew the bottom of the pouch by hand along the length of the beaded fringe with matching thread and a simple backstitch to secure in place. Be sure not to pull and gather the stitches. Machine stitch the remaining side seams with ½" seam allowance. For stability, sew a second seam very close to the first then trim away the excess fabric. Do not trim the tape that holds the beaded fringe.

3. Place the silk dupioni pieces right sides together. Pin around the perimeter and sew with a ½" seam allowance leaving a 3" opening along one side seam, as shown in Figure 4-11 at right. Backstitch at the beginning and end of the stitching. Sew a second seam very close to the first and trim away the excess fabric.

2. Do the same for all four edges. If the fabric slips, try basting it by hand before machine stitching. With wrong sides together, fold in half lengthwise and baste together close to the raw edges. Center the casing across the top of one of the velvet body pieces with right sides together.

3. Do the same for the other velvet body piece. Make sure the raw edges of the casing align with the raw edge of the top of the velvet body pieces. Sew with a ½" seam allowance.

4. Turn the velvet body right-side out and place inside the silk dupioni body with right sides together. The casing should be inside the bag sandwiched between the velvet and the silk dupioni. Sew around the top using a ½" seam allowance. Sew a second seam very close to the first and trim away the excess fabric.

5. Turn the bag right-side out through the 3" opening. Push the seam allowance inside the opening and slipstitch closed. Insert the lining inside the bag and finger-press the casing upright.

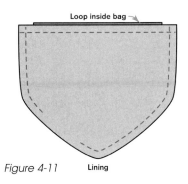

Figure 4-11

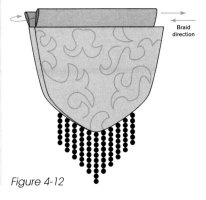

The soft Devoré velvet and glistening jet-black beads make this pouch well suited for a night at the symphony.

braid straps

1. Place a safety pin on one end of a braid and send through one casing then the other, as shown in Figure 4-12, and tie in a knot.

2. Do the same with the other braid, but start at the casing on the opposite side.

3. Pull the drawstrings from each end.

Figure 4-12

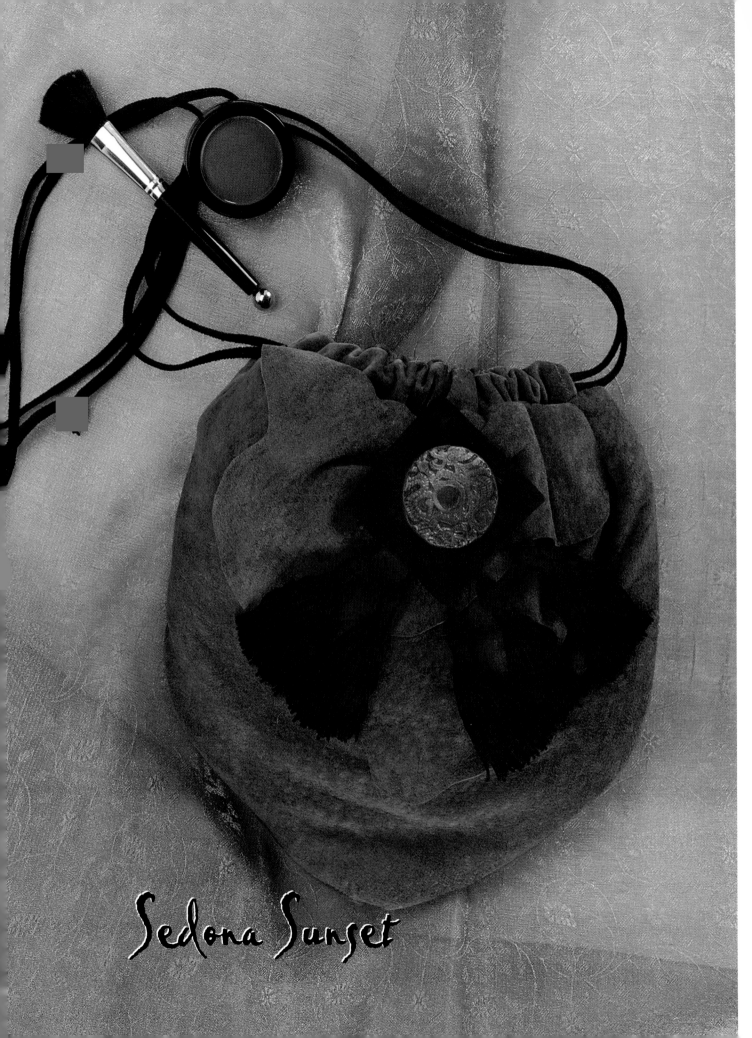

Sedona Sunset

The lightweight teal suede is supple and soft, so it needs a quilted lining to give it more shape and stability. The lime green silk dupioni is extremely lightweight, but quilting it with batting provides the body needed to fill out the shape. The raku button makes this purse really stand out. Raku is a ceramic technique and although these buttons are made from clay, they are extremely sturdy. The artists at Rama create raku buttons in various shapes, sizes, and vibrant colors. But the motifs imprinted are what make these buttons so special. A raku button pin was created specifically for this purse. It was placed on black suede then adorned with silken tassels to frame the beautiful fastener.

finished size
9½″ x 8½″

fabric and notions
¾-yard teal suede

¼-yard black suede

½-yard lime green silk dupioni

Air-Lite batting

56″ braided cord

Schmetz topstitch size 100 needle

Threads to match each fabric

Fabri-Tac®

Raku button

2¼″ cardboard square

5 3″ black tassels

Pin back

Safety pin

Patterns

prepare
1. Cut, as follows:
- two teal suede pieces of pattern #ONE-1 (body)
- two lime green silk dupioni pieces of pattern #ONE-1 (body)
- two Air-Lite batting of pattern #ONE-1 (body)
- two teal suede pieces of #ONE-2 (casing)
- one each teal suede pieces of patterns #ONE-3 and #ONE-4 (asymmetrical panels)
- two 28″ lengths rayon braid
- 3¼″ black suede square
- 2¼″ black suede square

2. Spray the adhesive on the wrong side of the silk dupioni pieces and place the wrong side down on the batting.

embellish
1. The silk dupioni lining is quilted with two strands of rayon threads. The sewing machine is threaded through the top with two spools of 30-weight Sulky rayon thread. Both threads are treated as one and sent through a Schmetz topstitch size 100 needle.

2. A design is traced onto quilting paper and pinned in place over the silk dupioni. Free-motion is used to follow the designs and then the paper is torn crisply away.

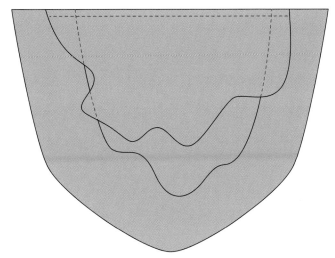

Figure 4-13

assemble
1. The assembly of the bag is the same as that for Black Tie and Tails, pages 37-39, with the addition of two asymmetrically cut panels of suede in the front.

2. Place the panels in the center of the bag, as shown in Figure 4-13, and pin in place at the top edge.

(continued)

Finished raku pin: Use it as bag adornment only, or remove it and try it on your favorite garment.

pin

1. Collect one 1½" raku button, five 3" tassels (measurement does not include the loop at the top, which can vary in length), a pin back, Fabri-Tac glue, and soft black suede.

2. Cut a 2¼" cardboard square.

3. Place the 3¼" black suede square right-side down (rough side) and draw a bead of glue in a 1" circle, as in Figure 4-14.

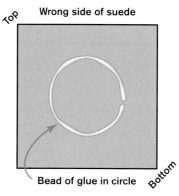

Wrong side of suede

Top

Bottom

Bead of glue in circle

Figure 4-14

4. Center the cardboard on the suede, as shown below in Figure 4-15.

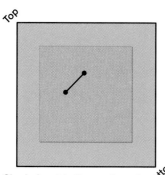

Shaded part is the cardboard. The button is sewn on the front.

Figure 4-15

5. Carefully draw a bead of glue along the edge of the suede square, as in Figure 4-16, and then fold all four corners toward the center.

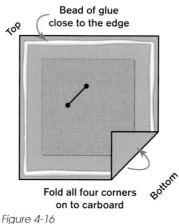

Top

Bead of glue close to the edge

Bottom

Fold all four corners on to carboard

Figure 4-16

6. Add more glue to the edge of the folded corners, as shown in Figure 4-17, and then fold all four sides toward the center. This creates mitered corners.

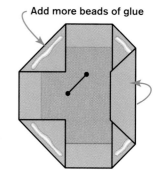

Add more beads of glue

Figure 4-17

7. Turn the square over, place the button in the center (turning the square on point so it is more like a diamond), and sew the button onto the suede, starting from the back of the cardboard, as shown.

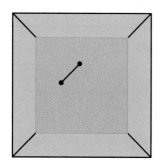

Figure 4-18

8. Referring to Figure 4-19, draw a bead of glue around the bottom corner of the diamond, place the five tassels spaced evenly apart, as shown, and glue them in place by the loop above the tassel. Press them lightly into the glue.

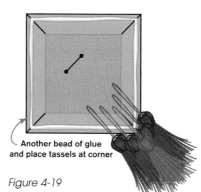

Another bead of glue and place tassels at corner

Figure 4-19

9. Draw another bead of glue around the suede square. Center the wrong side of the smaller suede square over the glue and press lightly. Glue the pin backing to the center, as in Figure 4-20, making sure that the direction of the pin maintains the raku on-point direction.

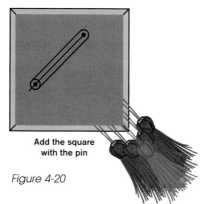

Add the square with the pin

Figure 4-20

Mystic Knot

The red silk matka, with its look of linen, is embellished with stenciled designs and drawn together with a rayon braid. The matka has a lot of body so instead of a casing, which would be difficult to gather up, rayon loops were used. The 100 percent cotton lining is printed with Japanese calligraphy called Kanji and quilted with gray thread. One side is stenciled with a Kanji symbol for "dream" and the other side a gold dragonfly.

finished size

9½" x 11"

fabric and notions

½-yard red silk matka

½-yard gray cotton print

Air-Lite batting

96" black braided cord

Threads to match each fabric

3 3"-long black tassels

Tsukineko Kanji stencil with Fabrico stamp pad or a laser-cut Mylar dragonfly stencil by Diane Ericson (#20 Bugs in Flight)

Dauber applicator

Lumiere® gold metallic paint

Paintbrush

Safety pin

16" square cardboard

Teflon pressing sheet

Iron

Spoons (for weights)

Patterns

prepare

1. Cut, as follows:
   - two red silk matka pieces of pattern #ONE-1 (body)
   - two gray cotton print pieces of pattern #ONE-1 (body)
   - two Air-Lite batting pieces of pattern #ONE-1 (body)
   - 12 5"-long pieces braid
   - two 18"-long pieces braid

embellish

Kanji Application

1. Lay the silk with the right side up. Peel the paper off the back of the Kanji stencil and center on the body.

2. Lightly gather the top of the body to see if your design will get lost in the folds. The stencil can still be moved. Press the stencil in place.

3. Dab the dauber in the inkpad and press over the stencil design. The slubby texture of the matka required two applications with five minutes to dry between applications.

4. When completely dry (about 20 minutes later), cover with the Teflon pressing sheet and press with a silk setting without steam to set the ink, for the result shown in the accompanying photo at right.

Press stenciled Kanji area with iron on silk setting to set the ink.

The auspicious golden dragonfly, symbol of prosperity, stops to rest on the Mystic Knot, symbol of protection. What a perfect combination for your valuables!

dragonfly application

1. Lay the silk with right side up on the cardboard.

2. Anchor the Mylar stencil in place on the fabric with some weights (spoons will do).

3. Dip the paintbrush in the Lumiere metallic paint and cover the stencil area with an even coat of paint.

4. Do not move the stencil for an hour.

5. Remove the stencil and let the paint dry for 24 hours.

6. Cover with the Teflon sheet and set with the heat of an iron. The finished look is shown in the photo at right.

Once the paint has dried for 24 hours, set the dragonfly with an iron.

assemble

1. Fold the loops in half and place across the top equal distances apart, as shown in Figure 4-21. Baste them in place on both body pieces. The loops take the place of the casing.

Figure 4-21

2. Group the three tassels together. With a needle and thread of the same color, baste them together, sewing through the horizontal threads that hold the tassel together, as shown in Figure 4-22. Hide the

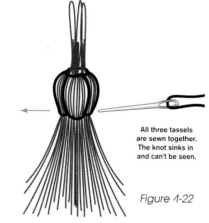

All three tassels are sewn together. The knot sinks in and can't be seen.

Figure 4-22

knot between the threads of the tassel. Place the tassel upside-down at the bottom center point.

3. Referring to Figure 4-23, assemble in the same manner as Black Tie and Tails, page 39.

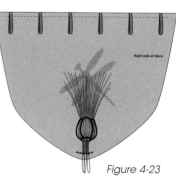

Right side of fabric

Figure 4-23

Weave the braids through the loops to create the drawstring top.

4. Send one of the 18″ braids through the loops, starting at one of the side seams of the bag, and then return to the starting point and tie the two ends together.

5. Repeat step 4 for the other braid, starting at the other side seam.

For the
Love of
Lavender

The multicolored cotton batik print and lavender linen bag is embellished with a green rayon fringe and coordinating rayon thread satin stitching in a zigzag pattern. The handle is made from the linen cut on the bias and filled with a cotton cord. The bottom is enforced with plastic canvas placed between the linen and lining. This can be a reversible bag, and is a smart addition for classic outfits.

finished size
8" x 9"

fabric and notions

1 yard lavender linen

½-yard cotton batik print

10" x 12" iron-on tricot stabilizer

Air-Lite batting

2 pieces 7" x 11" quilting paper

Zigzag quilting design

22" green rayon fringe

Sewing thread to match

Decorative 30- or 40-weight green rayon thread or poly embroidery thread

Fasturn

Fabri-Tac

Spray adhesive

2" x 9" plastic canvas

2 10"-long cotton cord strips

Teflon pressing sheet

Iron

Pins

Scissors

Patterns

prepare

1. Cut, as follows:
- two cotton batik pieces of pattern #TWO-1 (lining)
- two batting pieces of pattern #TWO-1 (lining)
- two cotton batik pieces of pattern #TWO-2, plus 2" extra*, around entire piece (upper body)
- two batting pieces of pattern #TWO-2 plus 2" extra* around entire piece (upper body)
- two stabilizer pieces of pattern #TWO-2 plus 2" extra* around entire piece (upper body)
- two lavender linen pieces of pattern #TWO-3 (lower body)
- two stabilizer pieces of pattern #TWO-3 (lower body)

2. Spray adhesive on the wrong sides of the pattern #TWO-1 cotton batik lining pieces and place on the batting.

3. Spray adhesive on the wrong sides of the pattern #TWO-2 cotton batik pieces cut and place on the batting.

4. Place the cotton batik/batting pieces on the tear away stabilizer and pin in several places.

5. Place the fusible side of the tricot stabilizer on the wrong side of the lavender linen pieces and press with the Teflon pressing sheets.

6. Make two copies of the zigzag design found on pattern #TWO-2 on quilting paper.

*The extra 2" is to allow for shrinkage during stitching. After the stitching is completed, the fabric will be re-cut with pattern #TWO-2.

embellish

1. Place a copy of the zigzag design on quilting paper on top of the batik-batting-stabilizer stack.

2. Pin through all layers. Do the same to create another identical stack.

3. Thread the sewing machine with the decorative thread.

4. Next, set up the machine for the satin stitching with a 3cm width. Try several widths and see which you prefer. Carefully follow the pattern lines and if it is difficult to turn the corners then stop and pivot, making sure to start again with a stitch on the inside of the corner.

5. When finished, tear away the stabilizer underneath and the quilting paper on top.

6. Re-cut the embellished pieces with pattern #TWO-2.

(continued)

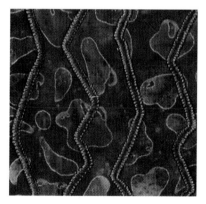

assemble

1. Place the embellished batik piece and the linen piece with right sides together, matching the notches. Sew with a ½" seam allowance.

Do the same for the other two pieces. Press the seams open.

2. Place these two batik/linen pieces with right sides together, pin side seams, and sew with a ½" seam allowance.

3. Trim away the excess batting from the seam allowances. Press the seams open.

4. Pin and sew the bottom with a ½" seam allowance, trim and press the seams open.

5. Finish the bottom by folding the corners of the bottom. Measure 1" in from the corner, pin across, and sew.

6. Face the points toward the center and then tack the points in place.

7. Place the two pieces of batik lining with right sides together. Pin. Sew the side seams and the bottom seam with a ½" seam allowance, trim, and press the seams open.

8. Finish the bottom in the same manner as for the bag's exterior, adding the plastic canvas for the bottom support when tacking the corners. The plastic canvas can be trimmed if it is too large.

9. Place the lining inside the bag with wrong sides together. Match side seam and the top edges and pin.

handles

1. Fold each 2½" x 10" linen strip lengthwise with right sides together. Place the folded edge along the ⅝" increment on the sewing machine throat plate. Backstitch to anchor when beginning and ending.

2. Use the Fasturn to turn the tubes right-side out while adding the cotton cord. Make sure both strips are the same length. On each end of the tubes, pull the cotton cords out a little and trim off ½", then slip them back into the tubes. This will keep the tubes flat where they are attached to the bag.

3. Fold each side of the bag in half and mark with a pin. Measure out 1½" in either direction from the pin and place pins at these locations. Remove the center pin. Place one end of the handle on each pin. Line up the tube handle edge with the top edge of the bag. Pin and baste in place ⅜" from the edge. Do this for both handles.

trim

1. Measure the perimeter of the top of the bag and add 1". Cut the 4" x 23" strip of periwinkle linen to that measurement. Fold in half with right sides together and sew the short ends with a ½" seam allowance.

2. Press the seam open. Fold the length of the strip in half with wrong sides together and press.

3. Referring to Figure 4-24, place the strip along the top edge of the bag with right sides together, making sure to align the raw edges of the strip with the raw edges of the top of the bag. Align the strip's seam with one of the side seams of the bag, pin in place, and sew across the top with a ½" seam allowance. Press the strip so it faces up.

4. Lower the strip and insert the 1" strip of batting in between. This will create a rounded trim matching the roundness of the handle. Turn the strip over the seam allowances to the other side. Have the folded edge of the strip meet the ½" seam that shows on the inside.

5. Pin in place and slipstitch by hand or stitch-in-the-ditch.

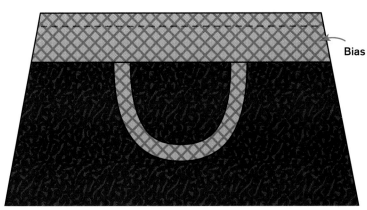

Figure 4-24

fringe

1. The rayon fringe has a flat straight edge on one side. Place the flat edge of the rayon fringe over the seam where the batik and the linen meet, as shown in Figure 4-25. Start at one of the side seams and go all the way around and overlap by ½". Cut away the excess.

2. Carefully draw a bead of glue along the seam line. Place the wrong side of the rayon fringe flat edge down on the glue and press in place.

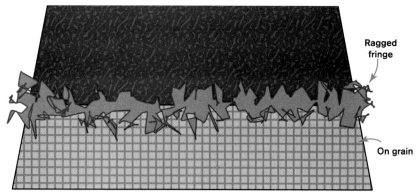

Ragged fringe

On grain

Figure 4-25

Attach the fringe.

A mélange of exquisite textures gives this bag character.

Rodeo Drive

The cowgirl and barbed wire cotton print are mixed with red and blue star fabric to create this cute Western-theme bag. Grommets are used as an embellishment application as well as a utilitarian method to thread the drawstrings.

finished size

8¼" x 9"

fabric and notions

¼-yard cowgirl cotton print

¼-yard barbed wire cotton print

1 yard blue star cotton print

2 11" x 13" iron-on craft fleece

⅛-yard red star cotton print

Sewing thread

Fasturn

Fabri-Tac

2" x 5" plastic canvas

14 size ⁷⁄₁₆" grommet sets (with setting tool)

Measuring tape

Iron

Erasable pen

Pins

Scissors

Patterns

prepare

1. Cut, as follows:
- two blue star cotton pieces of pattern #TWO-1 (lining)
- two fusible craft fleece pieces of pattern #TWO-1 (lining)
- two cowgirl cotton print pieces of pattern #TWO-2 (upper body)
- two barbed wire cotton print pieces of pattern #TWO-3 (lower body)
- two 2" x 15" red star cotton strips (drawstring straps)
- 4" x 7" blue star cotton (covers cross-stitch material)
- 3" x 23" bias strip blue star cotton (trim)

2. Place the cowgirl print and the barbed wire fabric with right sides together, matching notches. Pin and sew with a ½" seam allowance. Repeat for the remaining two fabric pieces.

3. Press the seams down towards the barbed wire fabric.

4. Place the wrong side of each piece with the fusible side of the craft fleece.

5. Press to adhere and treat as one.

assemble

1. Place the two cowgirl-barbed wire pieces with right sides together, pin the side seams, and sew with a ½" seam allowance. Trim away the excess batting from the seam allowances. Press the seams open.

2. Place the two blue star lining pieces with right sides together. Pin the side seams and sew with a ⅝" seam allowance. Trim the seams to ⅜" and press open. (This is not a reversible bag, so the lining is made slightly smaller.)

3. Place the lining inside the cowgirl/barbed wire piece with wrong sides together. Match the side seams and pin. Smooth out the lining and pin through all layers.

embellish

1. To mark the grommet placement for the drawstring, measure 1" down from the top edge of the bag and draw a light line with an erasable ink pen or fine chalk line all the way around the edge.

2. Fold the bag flat and measure 1¼" in from each side seam and make a vertical mark on the horizontal line. Measure the distance between the two vertical lines and divide by three and mark two more vertical lines dividing it into thirds. You will have four vertical lines marked for the grommets.

3. Read the directions on the grommet package. There is a front grommet and a back grommet. Turn the front grommet upside-down and center the hole over the cross marks made with the erasable pen. Using the erasable pen, trace the inside of the grommet hole. Do this for all four grommet markings on each side of the bag.

(continued)

4. Pin around each grommet marking. Using very sharp, pointed 4" scissors, cut out the holes that are marked with the erasable pen. Cut the first one a little smaller than the marking and test the fit of the grommet. If it does need to be larger, then cut around the circle making the hole larger and test the fit of the grommet again. It should be a little snug without pulling or distorting the fabric.

5. When you have found the right fit, cut the rest of the holes to the same size. Be sure to refer to the grommet directions because they may vary depending on the manufacturer variations. Now mark three more holes for the barbed wire portion on each side of the bag. Be sure not to place them too low.

6. Basically, you will be sending the front grommet through the front of the bag. The back grommet will slide over the protrusion of the front grommet from the inside of the bag. Depending on your application tool, the front and back will be pressed together.

trim

1. Measure the perimeter of the top of the bag and add 1".
2. Cut the 3" x 23" strip of blue star print to that measurement. Fold in half with right sides together and sew the short ends with a ½" seam allowance. Press the seam open.

3. Fold the length of the strip in half with wrong sides together and press. Place the strip around the top edge of the bag with right sides together. Align the raw edges of the strip with the bag top's raw edges. Align the strip seam with one of the side seams of the bag. Pin in place.

4. Sew across the top with a ½" seam allowance. Press the strip so it faces up. Fold the strip over the seam allowances to the inside to encase the raw edges. Match the strip's folded edge to the ½" stitching line that shows on the inside. Pin in place and slipstitch by hand or stitch-in-the-ditch.

drawstring

1. With right sides together, fold each red star strip in half lengthwise. Place the folded edge along the ⅝" marking on the sewing machine throat plate and sew the entire length to create a ⅝" seam allowance. Make sure the tension on your sewing machine is correct to avoid seams that break later.
2. Backstitch to secure at the beginning and end of each strip. Do not trim the seam allowances, as they help to add body to the drawstrings.

3. Turn right-side out with a Fasturn.
4. Begin threading the drawstring from one side of the bag by going in the first grommet, out the second, into the third, and out the fourth, as shown in Figure 4-26. Carry the drawstring around the side seam and repeat the threading on the other side in the same manner.

5. Referring to Figure 4-27, join the drawstring ends by first tucking one end in upon itself to create a finished edge. Next, tuck the opposite raw end into the finished opening. Slipstitch the edge to join the drawstring into a circle.
6. Repeat the above steps for the other drawstring.

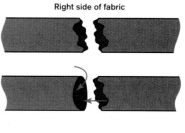

Right side of fabric

How the drawstring ends are finished (optional)

Figure 4-27

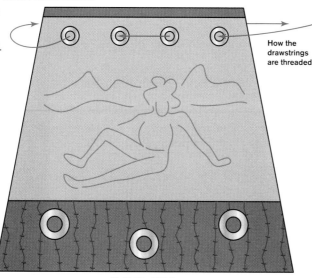

How the drawstrings are threaded

Figure 4-26

Right side of fabric

finish

1. Turn the bag inside out and place the fronts of the bag together. Sew from one side seam to the other across the bottom with a ½" seam allowance. Trim the excess fleece from the seam allowance. Press the seam open. Finish the bottom by folding the corners, measuring 1" down, and sewing across.

2. Tack the points to the bottom of the bag. Cover the plastic canvas with the 4" x 7" blue star fabric.

3. Run a bead of glue over the edges of the fabric and turn them over the edge of the plastic canvas. Press in place.

4. Run a bead of glue near the perimeter on the wrong side and then press it onto the bottom of the bag, making sure that the seams in the bottom of the bag are covered.

Take this grommet-studded pouch with you when you're out lookin' for cowboys.

Safari Satchel

● This cotton safari border print is embellished with three gold dimensional giraffes and embellished with rayon thread using a satin stitch. It is lined with a reversible zebra print embellished with gold metallic thread and finished with twisted rattan handles. ●

finished size
8¼" x 8½"

fabric and notions

½-yard safari border cotton print

½-yard zebra cotton print

Air-Lite batting

1 yard solid black cotton fabric

2 11" x 13" pieces tear-away stabilizer

40" rayon braid

Sewing thread to match fabrics

Rayon and metallic thread*

Plastic canvas:
- 2" x 5" piece
- 2 7" x 5" pieces

Animal embellishment with holes

Spray adhesive

Pins

Scissors

Patterns

*I used either gold Sulky Sliver or Superior Thread Glitter.

prepare

1. Cut, as follows:
- two safari border print pieces of pattern #TWO-1 (bag body)
- two zebra print pieces of pattern #TWO-1 (lining)
- four batting pieces of pattern #TWO-1
- 4" x 23" black cotton bias strip (trim)
- four 9" strips rayon braid (with knotted ends)

2. Spray adhesive on the wrong side of the safari border print and place on the Air-Lite batting.

3. Spray the adhesive on the wrong side of the zebra print and place on the Air-Lite batting. Treat the fabric-batting pieces as single units from this point on.

embellish

1. For the safari border print, place the tear-away stabilizer under one of the safari border print/batting pieces. Pin through all layers.

2. Satin stitch with a coordinating color, using rayon and/or metallic thread, between two of the border designs, as shown in Figure 4-27. Instead of sewing a straight line, turn the fabric slightly while sewing to create an elongated zigzag line or use one of the decorative stitches available on your sewing machine. Do the same for the remaining fabric/batt unit.

3. For the zebra print reversible lining, thread the machine with gold metallic thread and switch to the free-motion sewing machine foot. Quilt both of the zebra print/batting pieces with a meandering, all-over design.

(continued)

Figure 4-27

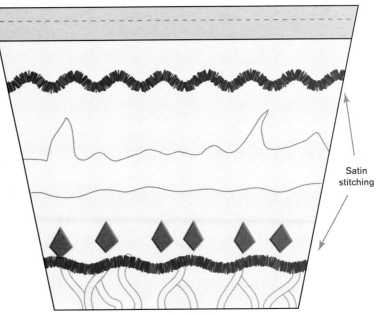

Satin stitching

Right side of fabric

The handle is attached by tying knots in the fabric loops.

assemble

1. Place the two safari border print pieces with right sides together. Pin the side seams and sew with a ½" seam allowance. Trim the excess batting from the seam allowance.

2. Sew across the bottom with a ½" seam and trim the excess batting. Fold the two corners at the bottom, measure 1" down, and sew across. Turn right-side out.

3. Place the 2" x 5" plastic canvas in the bottom.

4. Repeat steps 1 and 2 for the zebra print reversible lining. Insert the zebra print lining inside the safari border print bag with wrong sides together. Smooth to fit.

5. Place the plastic canvas between the two bags on each side. Hand-sew the embellishment to the front of the bag and tack the plastic in place at the same time.

6. For the rayon braid ties, find the zebra lining bag's center front and place a pin. For a "D" shaped handle, measure the distance between the inside of the handles. Divide that measurement in half. Use that measurement in either direction of that center pin and place two pins. Remove the center pin. Repeat for the other side of the bag.

7. Fold the four 9" braids in half. Place the folded edge along the top edge of the bag where it is marked with the four pins. Baste the braids ½" away from the fold, as shown in Figure 4-28.

8. For the black trim, measure the perimeter of the bag's top and add

1". Cut/reduce the length of the 4" x 23" strip of black fabric to that measurement. Fold the strip in half with right sides together and sew the short ends with a ½" seam allowance. Press the seam open.

9. Fold the length of the strip in half with wrong sides together and press. Place the strip around the top edge of the safari border print bag with right sides together. Align the raw edges of the strip with the raw edges at the top of the bag and place the strip's seam joining at one of the side seams of the bag. Pin in place.

10. Sew around the top with a ½" seam allowance. Press the strip so it faces up.

11. Fold the strip over the seam allowances to the inside to encase the raw edges. Match the strip's folded edge to the ½" stitching line that shows on the inside. Pin in place and slipstitch by hand or stitch-in-the-ditch.

12. Tie double-knots around the handles with each pair of ties, as shown in the photo at top left of this page.

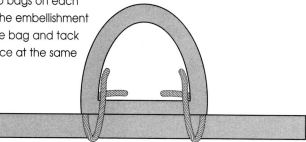

Figure 4-28

View from inside
The bag shows where the ties orginate—from under the trim

Calligraphy
Tote

This large tote with warm, rich earth tones and sweeping Japanese calligraphy appeals to everyone. It is lined with an Asian motif toile and enhanced with faux marble handles. You can reverse it for another look!

finished size

12½" x 14½"

fabric and notions

½-yard brown calligraphy upholstery-weight fabric

⅔-yard Asian motif toile cotton

Air-Lite batting

2 20" x 14" fusible craft fleece

2 round faux marble handles

Adhesive spray

Sewing thread to match fabric

Fasturn

Black rayon thread

4" x 9" plastic canvas

Pins

Scissors

Patterns

note

More fabric may be required for large motifs, depending on the repeat and centering.

prepare

1. Cut, as follows:
- two brown calligraphy fabric pieces of pattern #THREE-1
- two Asian motif toile pieces of pattern #THREE-1
- three 20" x 40" strips of Asian motif toile
- two batting pieces of pattern #THREE-1
- two craft fleece pieces of pattern #THREE-1. (Trim the seam allowances from the fleece.)

2. Place the wrong side of the brown calligraphy fabric with the fusible side of the fleece and press. Repeat for the remaining fabric and fleece.

3. Lightly spray the wrong side of the Asian toile, place on the batting, and smooth in place. Repeat for the remaining fabric and batting. These two pieces will be quilted and then re-cut with pattern #THREE-1.

embellish

1. To quilt both pieces of the Asian toile-batting, thread the machine with black rayon thread and set the machine for free-motion.

2. Use a meandering stitch, a favorite quilting design, or outline quilt the design motifs.

3. To make the ties, sew a stay-stitch around the curve of the circle ⅜" from the raw edge on all four pieces.

4. Fold and pin the three long strips of Asian toile in half lengthwise with right sides together. Sew the length of the three long strips of Asian toile fabric with a ½" seam allowance. Cut these strips into 20 5½" lengths. Sew across the width of each small tube and turn right-side out.

5. Pin the ties in pairs. Place them around the curve of the Asian toile fabric/batting piece as marked on the pattern. The raw edge of the ties should align with the raw edge of the curve. Baste them in place, as shown in Figure 4-29. Repeat on the other Asian toile fabric/batting piece.

Figure 4-29

Right side of fabric

assemble

1. Place the two pieces of brown calligraphy fabric with right sides together and pin. Sew the side seams with a ½" seam allowance. Trim the excess fleece from the seam allowance. Press the seams open.

2. Sew across the bottom of the bag, trim, and press seams open. Fold the corners, measure 2" down, and sew across.

3. Place the two pieces of quilted Asian toile/batting with right sides together. Pin. Sew the side seams with a ½" seam allowance. Trim the excess batting from the seam allowances. Press the seams open.

4. Sew across the bottom of the bag leaving a 5" opening in the center. Trim and press the seams open. Fold the corners, measure down 2", and sew across.

5. Turn the brown calligraphy bag right-side out. Place it inside the Asian toile with right sides together.

6. Sew across the tops and around the curves with a ½" seam allowance. Reinforce the seam by sewing over the existing seam once more.

7. Trim the seam allowance to ¼" and cut away the excess batting from the seam allowance.

8. Clip around the curves every ½" up to the seam, but not through the stitching; this allows the fabric to have a smooth, curved edge when turned.

9. Turn the bag right-side out through the 5" opening in the Asian toile.

10. Use a point turner to fill out the corner near the curves. Place the plastic canvas in the bottom of the bag between the brown calligraphy fabric and the Asian toile. Slipstitch the opening closed.

11. Position the handle in the curve and tie the ends in place with a double-knot with each set of two ties. Do the same for the other handle.

The reverse of the Calligraphy Tote takes on a whole new look, essentially creating two bags for the price of one.

Bold strokes of Asian calligraphy or rich toile: Either way, the faux marble handles make this reversible say "classy."

Jungle Book

This irresistible design of monkeys with bow ties and hats went well with the woven grass fabric and round bamboo handles. Another matching floral fabric is used as the lining as well as for the zippered compartment inside.

finished size

13" x 12"

fabric and notions

½-yard monkey print fabric

⅔-yard woven grass fabric

⅔-yard floral fabric

½-yard buckram

2 20" x 14" fusible craft fleece

2 round bamboo handles

9" zipper

Sewing thread to match fabric

4" x 9" piece plastic canvas

Zipper foot

Fasturn

Pins

Scissors

Measuring tape

Iron

Patterns

note

A specialty zipper with larger teeth makes it easier to zip and unzip the compartment.

prepare

1. Cut, as follows:
- two monkey print pieces of pattern #THREE-1 (body)
- two floral pieces of pattern #THREE-1 (lining)
- two buckram pieces of pattern #THREE-1
- two fleece pieces of pattern #THREE-1
- four woven grass pieces of pattern #THREE-2 (trim)
- four floral pieces of pattern #THREE-3 (zippered compartment)

2. Place the wrong side of the monkey fabric to the fusible side of the fleece. Trim ⅝" off along the top edge of the fleece. Do the same for the other monkey fabric piece. Press to fuse the monkey fabric to the fleece.

3. Place the wrong side of the floral fabric with the buckram, pin together, and treat as one. Do the same for the other buckram piece.

4. Sew a stay-stitch around the curve of the circle, ⅜" from the raw edge on all four body pieces.

zippered compartment

1. Place two of the compartment pieces with right sides together and sew across the top with a ½" seam allowance, as shown in Figure 4-30. Press the seams open. Do the same for the other two pieces.

ties

1. Fold and pin the three long strips of woven grass fabric in half lengthwise with right sides together. Sew the length of the three long strips of woven grass fabric with a ½" seam allowance.

2. Cut this strip into 20 5½" lengths.

3. Sew across the width of each small tube.

4. Turn right-side out with a Fasturn.

5. Pin the ties in pairs and then place them around the curve of the floral fabric-buckram piece as marked on the pattern. The raw edge of the ties should align with the raw edge of the curve. Baste them in place. Do the same for the other piece.

(continued)

One of the two sets of two fabrics placed together and sewn across the top.

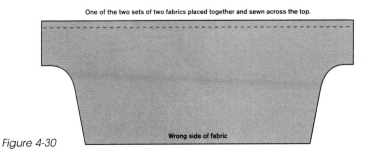

Figure 4-30

Wrong side of fabric

2. Place these two seamed pieces with right sides together, matching the seams, and pin through the seam line in several places. Mark a 9" length that is centered on the pinned seam. Sew along that seam line from the edge of the fabric to the 9" marking. Do the same from the other edge.

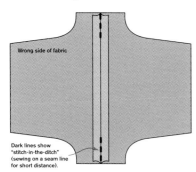

Wrong side of fabric

Dark lines show "stitch-in-the-ditch" (sewing on a seam line for short distance).

Figure 4-31

3. Now flip the top layer on the left over to the right and flip the bottom right layer to the left. This will result in a finished opening on both sides. Press.

4. Place the zipper under the opening. Pin the opening around the entire zipper.

5. Topstitch around the zipper opening, as shown in Figure 4-32.

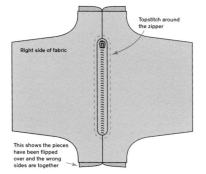

Right side of fabric

Topstitch around the zipper

This shows the pieces have been flipped over and the wrong sides are together

Figure 4-32

6. Referring to Figure 4-33, unzip the zipper opening and fold the compartment piece in half with the wrong side of the zipper at the top of the fold. Place the bottom edges together and sew with a ½" seam allowance. Sew the curved sides with a ½" seam allowance.

7. Trim the seams and clip all curves.

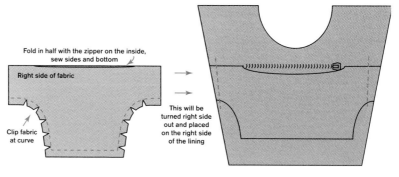

Fold in half with the zipper on the inside, sew sides and bottom

Right side of fabric

Clip fabric at curve

This will be turned right side out and placed on the right side of the lining

Figure 4-33

8. Turn right-side out through the un-zipped opening. This piece will later be used as indicated in Figure 4-34.

Figure 4-34

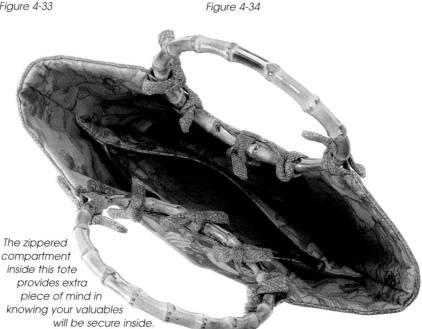

The zippered compartment inside this tote provides extra piece of mind in knowing your valuables will be secure inside.

assemble

1. Place the two pieces of monkey fabric with right sides together and pin then sew the side seams with a ½" seam allowance. Press the seams open.

2. Sew across the bottom of the bag and press the seams open. Fold the corners, measure 2" down and sew across.

3. Place the two pieces of floral fabric-buckram with right sides together. Place the zippered compartment in between as marked on the pattern. This will cause the lining to pull in and gap,

and this is OK. Pin and sew the side seams with a ½" seam allowance. Trim away the excess buckram and excess thickness of the zippered compartment from the seam allowance. Press the seams open.

4. Sew across the bottom of the bag, trim and press seams open. Fold the corners, measure down 2", and sew across.

5. Place the floral lining bag inside the monkey fabric bag with wrong sides together. Place the 4"x 9" plastic canvas in the bottom of the bag between the monkey fabric and the floral lining.

trim

1. Place two woven grass pieces with right sides together. Pin and sew the sides with a ½" seam allowance. Do the same for the other two.

2. Trim the seams to ¼" and press the seams open.

3. Place these two large trim pieces with right sides together, pin along the bottom edge, and sew with a ½" seam allowance. Trim to ¼" and clip around the curve up to the seam, as in Figure 4-35.

4. Turn right-side out and press with wrong sides together. Baste by hand along the finished edge.

5. Referring to Figure 4-36, place the trim on the floral lining with right sides together. Align all the raw edges at the top and side seams. Pin in place and sew across the top and around curves with a ½" seam allowance. Reinforce seams at the corners by sewing over the existing seam for 2" in either direction of the corner. Trim the seam to ¼". Clip the corner on the diagonal and also clip the curve up to the seam. Fold the trim over to the monkey fabric side and press. Topstitch close to the edge (where basted) through all layers.

6. Place the handle in the curve and tie them in a double-knot with each set of ties, as shown in the accompanying photo at right, and repeat for the other handle.

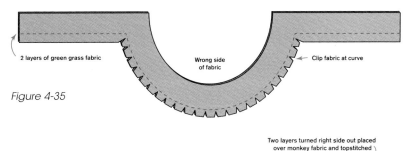

2 layers of green grass fabric   Wrong side of fabric   Clip fabric at curve

Figure 4-35

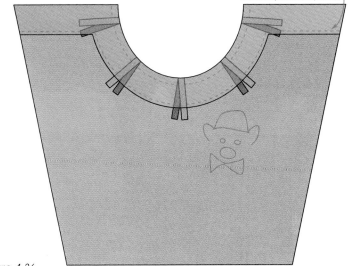

Two layers turned right side out placed over monkey fabric and topstitched

Figure 4-36

Right side of fabric

Use double-knots tie the handle to the bag's body.

Rue des
Francs-Bourgeois

This large, classy tote bag was made with the same pattern as the previous bags simply by eliminating the circular cutout. Brown leopard chiffon was used with a luscious, full feather boa. A hidden flap with a magnetic snap closure helps to hold the bag shape as well provide some security.

finished size

13" x 12"

fabric and notions

½-yard leopard fabric

½-yard black print fabric

½-yard solid black fabric

Fusible craft fleece:
- 9 x 5" piece
- 2 20" x 14" pieces

Air-Lite batting

2 20" x 18" pieces fusible web

40" strip 1"-diameter round cotton cord

1 set magnetic snaps

3" square fusible interfacing

4 purse feet

Sewing thread to match fabric

Plastic canvas:
- 4" x 9" piece
- 2 9" x 12" pieces

36" brown feather boa

Fasturn

Pins

Scissors

Iron

Measuring tape

Patterns

note

This sheer leopard print fabric needed to be backed with fleece for a smooth, sturdy body. Placing the sheer fabric on white fusible craft fleece would have changed the richness of the color, so fusible web and a brown fleece (used for creating clothing) were used. Don't be intimidated by sheer fabrics. Once bonded to fleece or batting, they are easy to work with.

prepare

1. Place the fusible web on the wrong side of the leopard fabric. Press. Peel off the backing paper and place the wrong side of the leopard print onto the fleece. Press. Repeat for the remaining leopard fabric. Be sure to use the Teflon pressing sheet.

2. Lightly spray the wrong side of the black print fabric and place on the Air-Lite batting. Do the same for the other fabric and batting. Select a favorite design and use free-motion to quilt the two pieces.

3. Cut, as follows:
- two leopard-fleece pieces of pattern #THREE-1 (bag body)
- two black print-batting pieces of pattern #THREE-1 (lining)
- two solid black pieces of pattern #THREE-4 (flap)
- two fleece pieces of pattern #THREE-4 (flap)
- two 2" x 21" solid black bias strips (handles)
- 2" x 35" solid black bias strip (trim)

assemble

1. Place the two leopard-fleece pieces with right sides together. Pin the side seams and sew with a ½" seam allowance. Trim the seams to ¼" and cut away the excess fleece from the seam allowance. Press seams open.

2. Sew across the bottom with a ½" seam allowance, trim, and press seams open. Fold the corners, measure 2" down, and sew across. Repeat for the remaining corner.

3. Face corner points toward the center.

4. Turn the bag right-side out and insert the 4" x 9" plastic canvas in the bottom of the bag.

5. Place the two black print-batting pieces with right sides together. Pin the side seams and sew with a ½" seam allowance. Trim to ¼" and press the seams open. Sew across the bottom, trim, and press.

6. Fold the corners, measure down 2" and sew across. Face corner points toward the center and tack in place.

7. Add metal purse feet to the bottom of the leopard print bag, as instructed on page 17.

(continued)

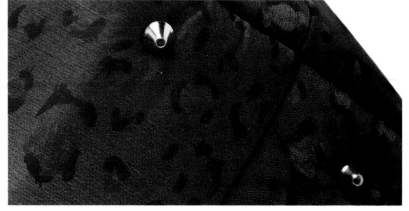

Add metal purse feet to the bottom to allow the purse to stand on its own.

snap and flap

1. Mark the placement for the magnetic snap on the black print-batting piece (check pattern). Make two small holes for one side of the magnetic snap where indicated.

2. Send the two metal prongs through the holes and bend flat to the side.

3. Place the lining bag inside the leopard print bag with wrong sides together.

4. Place the 9" x 12" plastic canvas pieces in the front and back of the bag, between the bag and lining. Pin all around the top edge of the bag through all layers.

5. Mark the placement for the magnetic snap on the right side of one of the black flap pieces. Trim the ½" seam allowance from the fusible fleece flap piece.

6. Center and fuse the fleece to the wrong side of the black fabric flap piece with the snap location marked.

7. Make two small holes for one side of the magnetic snap, where indicated.

8. Send the two metal prongs through the holes and bend flat to the side. Place the two flap pieces with right sides together.

9. Sew around the sides and curved front with a ½" seam allowance. Trim to ¼" and clip the curve up to the seam.

10. Turn right-side out and press.

11. Place a pin at the center of the back of the bag (opposite the first half of the magnetic snap). Place a pin in the center of the flap end with the raw edges. Place the flap on the outside of the back of the bag, matching the pins, and pin in place. Make sure the side of the flap with the magnetic snap is facing the leopard print or it will end up on the wrong side of the flap when everything is reversed. Baste in place.

handles

1. Place the two long strips 2" x 21" with right sides together and pin.

2. Place the folded edge along the ⅝" marking on the sewing machine's throat plate. That will create a ⅜" seam.

3. Cut the 40" cotton cord in half.

4. Turn the black fabric strips right-side out with the Fasturn, filling the strips with cotton cording at the same time. Check to make sure both tubes are the same length. Pull out and cut off ½" of cotton cord from each end of the handles.

5. Pin mark the center front and back of the bag. Measure 3" out in either direction and pin mark.

6. Remove the center pins. Place the handles inside the bag against the lining. Pin first and then baste in place.

finish

1. Fold the 35"-long strip in half with right sides together and sew the short ends with a ½" seam allowance. Trim to ¼" and press the seam open.

2. Place the bias trim along the top edge of the outside of the purse with right sides together, as shown in Figure 4-37.

3. Pin and then sew with a ½" seam allowance.

4. Turn the bias trim up and then over to the inside of the bag to encase the raw edges. Turn the bias strip edges under and pin. Slipstitch in place or stitch-in-the-ditch.

5. Turn the flap up and topstitch along the back edge of the flap to attach it to the black trim under it. Sew slowly through all thicknesses.

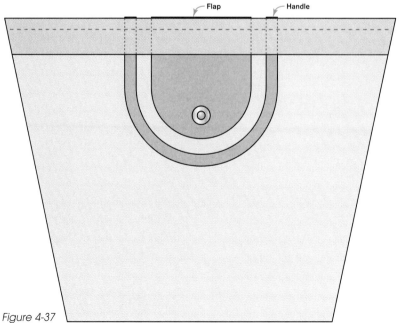

Figure 4-37

embellish

1. The boa is stitched in place by hand in place with doubled matching thread, as shown in Figure 4-38. Feel for the inner core of the feather boa. Start sewing from a side seam and tack the feather boa to the black trim edge of the bag.

Use loose, long stitches through the core of the feather boa and then through the top of the black trim. Repeat until you return to the beginning and overlap the boa an inch.

2. Cut away the excess boa.

Stitch feather boa in place by hand.

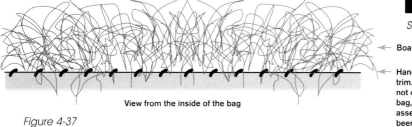

← **Boa**

← Handstitch boa to trim. (The trim is not on the actual bag, but it's easy to assemble, so it has been added to instrutions.)

View from the inside of the bag

Figure 4-37

"Bonjour, enchantez!"

Waikiki Sling

● Perfect for a trip to the beach or a stroll along the shops. Tuck in a travel guide and some sunglasses, and you're off! ●

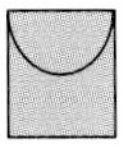

finished size

8" x 8½"

fabric and notions

- ¼-yard each of eight assorted cotton print fabrics
- 1 yard cotton print fabric
- Air-Lite batting
- Sewing thread to match the fabric
- Decorative rayon or metallic thread
- Free-motion quilting foot
- Pins
- Scissors
- Decorative button
- Patterns

note

Create the quilted fabric first, and then cut the bag pattern. In the sample, four different fabrics were repeated, but feel free to use up to eight fabrics. Make the straps longer or shorter, depending on how you will carry it.

prepare

1. Cut, on the cross-grain, one 1½" x 33" strip from each of the eight cotton print fabrics.

2. Sew the eight assorted cotton print strips together, side-by-side, with a ¼" seam. Press all the seams to one side in the same direction.

3. Cut 10" off the length, as shown in Figure 4-39, and place it perpendicular to the eight-piece strip. Place right sides together and sew with a ¼" seam. Press the seam to the side.

4. Place pattern #FOUR-1 over the right side of the pieced fabric. The two "clip" markings on the pattern shows where the flap begins. Place that "clip" part of the pattern so it falls 1½" below the last horizontal seam, as shown in Figure 4-40.

5. Cut, as follows:

- one pieced fabric piece of pattern #FOUR-1* (bag body)
- one batting piece of pattern #FOUR-1* (lining)
- one cotton print piece of pattern #FOUR-1* (lining)
- 2" x 25" cotton print bias strip (strap)
- 2" x 35" cotton print bias strip (strap)
- 2" x 4" cotton print bias strip (loop)
- 2" x 17" cotton print bias strip (flap trim)

*Make a ½" clip at each "clip" marking.

(continued)

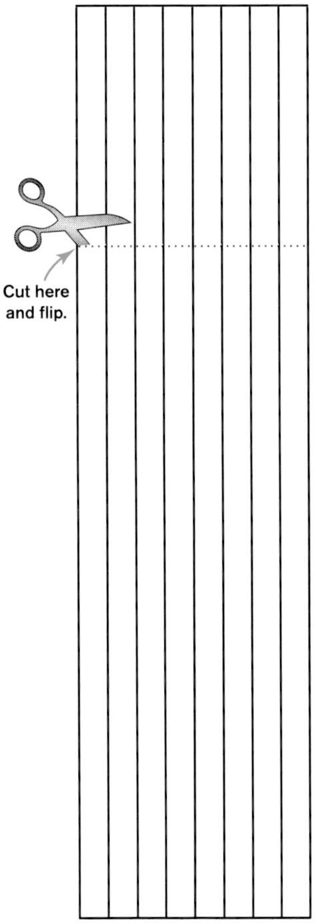

Cut here and flip.

Figure 4-39

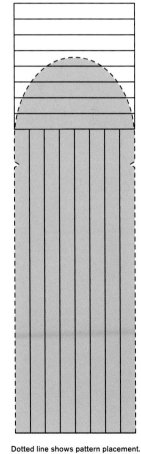

Dotted line shows pattern placement.

Figure 4-40

assemble

1. Place the pieced fabric and lining with right sides together. Place the batting underneath the lining. Pin through all layers. Sew the short straight edge opposite the flap. Sew with a ½" seam allowance and trim to ¼", as shown in Figure 4-41.

2. Flip the pieced fabric over to the other side of the batting. Press the finished seam.

3. Align all the layers and pin in several places.

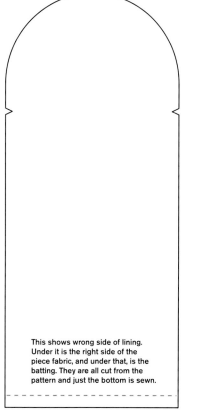

This shows wrong side of lining. Under it is the right side of the piece fabric, and under that, is the batting. They are all cut from the pattern and just the bottom is sewn.

Figure 4-41

embellish

1. Because the quilting will be seen from both sides of the bag, fill the bobbin with the same decorative thread as used for the top thread.

2. Attach the free-motion foot.

3. Quilt with meandering lines, as in Figure 4-42, or use a favorite quilting design.

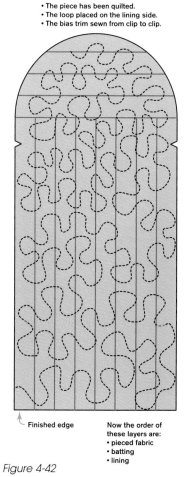

• The piece has been quilted.
• The loop placed on the lining side.
• The bias trim sewn from clip to clip.

Finished edge

Now the order of these layers are:
• pieced fabric
• batting
• lining

Figure 4-42

flap

1. Fold the loop strip in half with right sides together. The dimensions will be 1" x 4". Press.

2. Open the strip and bring both edges to meet at the center fold. Press.

3. Using the decorative thread in the sewing machine and bobbin, sew close to the two folded edges.

4. Bring the two ends together and pin in the center of the curved flap as indicated on the pattern.

5. Fold the beginning of the trim strip back with wrong sides together to start with a finished edge and place at the clip, as in Figure 4-43. Align and pin the strip edge with the strip pieced flap edge to the other clip. Be sure to "ease" the bias strip over the curve. Warning: If the bias strip is pulled taut, it may cause the flap to "cup" instead of laying flat.

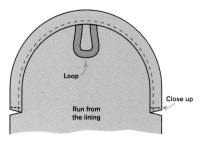

Optional

Inside

Fold

Figure 4-43

6. Fold the end of the strip fabric back with wrong sides together and cut away the excess strip. Sew with a ½" seam allowance, as shown in Figure 4-44. Turn the strip over to the lining side and tuck the raw edge under and have that folded edge meet the seam line. Topstitch with the same decorative threads.

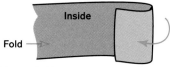

Loop

Close up

Run from the lining

Figure 4-44

straps

1. Fold each of the two strap strips in half lengthwise with wrong sides together and press.

2. Open the fold and place the long edge of the strip to meet the inside of the fold, as shown in Figure 4-45. Do the same for the other edge.

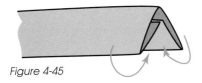

Figure 4-45

3. Fold the ends of the straps under.

4. Place one end of the strap at the bottom corner of the bag "sandwiching" all of the side seam layers. Pin up the side seam to the "clip" and then continue pinning to the end of the strap. Do the same for the other side.

5. With the decorative thread still in the machine and the bobbin, topstitch close to the edge of the straps sewing through all layers, as shown in Figure 4-46. Make sure to catch the edge of the strap underneath. Sew the length of both straps.

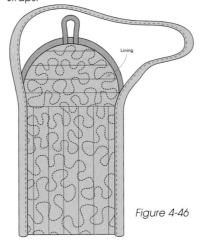

Figure 4-46

6. Tie a double-knot with the two straps.

note

You may want to use a bias tape maker for the straps and trim. Purchase one that will produce a 1"-wide bias tape that will be folded in half. Follow the manufacturer's directions. Some bias tape makers require that you use their fabric width increments, so be sure to use that measurement.

finish

1. Bring the straight finished edge up to meet the clip mark so the lining is on the inside. Pin the side seams on the pieced side of the bag. Sew with a ¼" seam.

2. Turn the bag so the lining side is facing out. Fold the corners, measure 1" down, and sew across. Tack the corners to the bottom of the bag.

3. Turn the bag right-side out.

4. Add a special button to create the effect that is shown in the accompanying photo below.

Add a whimsical button, like this cute little fish, for a swimmingly perfect touch.

Slivers of color from the sky, sea, and land to remind you of a perfect day in paradise.

Espresso Bar

This is a longer version of the Waikiki Sling, which is detailed on pages 68-71. All the directions are the same except the strips for the body of the bag are 4″ longer.

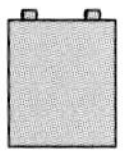

finished size

11″ x 8″

fabric and notions

¼-yard each of eight
cotton print fabrics

1 yard cotton print fabric

Air-Lite batting

Sewing thread to match the fabric

Decorative rayon
or metallic thread

Pins

Scissors

Decorative button and tassel

Patterns

prepare

1. Cut, on the cross-grain, one
1½″ x 38″ strip from each of the
eight cotton print fabrics.

2. Sew the eight assorted cotton
print strips together, side-by-side,
with a ¼″ seam. Press all the seams
to one side in the same direction.

3. Cut 6″ off the length, as in Figure
4-47, and place it perpendicular to
the eight-piece strip. Place right
sides together and sew with a ¼″
seam. Press the seam to the side.

4. Place pattern #FOUR-1 over the
right side of the pieced fabric. The
two "clip" markings on the pattern
shows where the flap begins. Place
that "clip" part of the pattern so it
falls 1½″ below the last horizontal
seam, as shown in Figure 4-48.

5. Cut, as follows:
- one pieced fabric piece of
  pattern #FOUR-1* (bag body)
- one batting piece of pattern
  #FOUR-1* (lining)
- one cotton print piece of
  pattern #FOUR-1* (lining)
- 2″ x 25″ cotton print bias strip
  (strap)
- 2″ x 35″ cotton print bias strip
  (strap)
- 2″ x 4″ cotton print bias strip
  (loop)
- 2″ x 17″ cotton print bias strip
  (flap trim)

*Make a ½″ clip at each "clip"
marking.

assemble

1. Place the pieced fabric and lining with right sides together. Place the
batting underneath the lining. Pin through all layers. Sew the short straight
edge opposite the flap. Sew with a ½″ seam allowance and trim to ¼″, as
shown in Figure 4-49.

2. Flip the pieced fabric over to the other side of the batting. Press the
finished seam. Align all the layers and pin in several places.

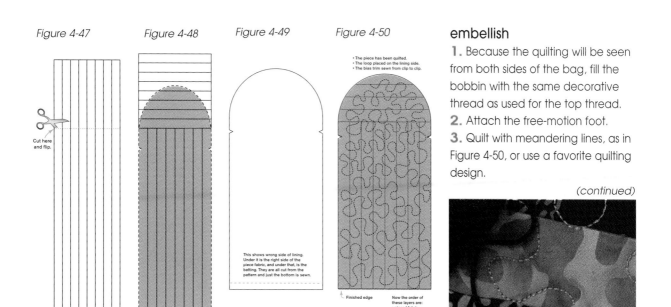

Figure 4-47

Cut here
and flip.

Figure 4-48

Dotted line shows pattern placement.

Figure 4-49

This shows wrong side of lining.
Under it is the right side of the
piece fabric, and under that, is the
batting. They are all cut from the
pattern and just the bottom is sewn.

Figure 4-50

• The piece has been quilted.
• The loop placed on the lining side.
• The bias trim sewn from clip to clip.

Finished edge

Now the order of
these layers are:
• pieced fabric
• batting
• lining

embellish

1. Because the quilting will be seen
from both sides of the bag, fill the
bobbin with the same decorative
thread as used for the top thread.

2. Attach the free-motion foot.

3. Quilt with meandering lines, as in
Figure 4-50, or use a favorite quilting
design.

(continued)

flap

1. Fold the loop strip in half with right sides together. The dimensions will be 1" x 4". Press.

2. Open the strip and bring both edges to meet at the center fold. Press.

3. Using the decorative thread in the sewing machine and bobbin, sew close to the two folded edges.

4. Bring the two ends together and pin in the center of the curved flap as indicated on the pattern.

5. Fold the beginning of the trim strip back with wrong sides together to start with a finished edge and place at the clip, as in Figure 4-51. Align and pin the strip edge with the strip pieced flap edge to the other clip. Be sure to "ease" the bias strip over the curve. Warning: If the bias strip is pulled taut, it may cause the flap to "cup" instead of laying flat.

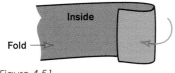

Optional

Inside

Fold

Figure 4-51

6. Fold the end of the strip fabric back with wrong sides together and cut away the excess strip. Sew with a ½" seam allowance, as shown in Figure 4-52.

7. Turn the strip over to the lining side and tuck the raw edge under and have that folded edge meet the seam line. Topstitch with decorative thread.

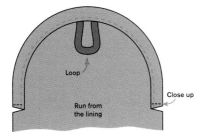

Loop

Close up

Run from the lining

Figure 4-52

straps

1. Fold each of the two strap strips in half lengthwise with wrong sides together and press.

2. Open the fold and place the long edge of the strip to meet the inside of the fold, as shown in Figure 4-53. Do the same for the other edge.

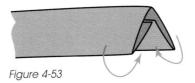

Figure 4-53

3. Fold the ends of the straps under.

4. Place one end of the strap at the bottom corner of the bag "sandwiching" all of the side seam layers. Pin up the side seam to the "clip" and then continue pinning to the end of the strap. Do the same for the other side.

5. With the decorative thread still in the machine and the bobbin, topstitch close to the edge of the straps sewing through all layers, as shown in Figure 4-54. Make sure to catch the edge of the strap underneath. Sew the length of both straps.

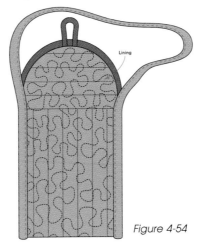

Lining

Figure 4-54

6. Tie a double-knot with the two straps.

finish

1. Bring the straight finished edge up to meet the clip mark so the lining is on the inside. Pin the side seams on the pieced side of the bag. Sew with a ¼" seam.

2. Turn the bag so the lining side is facing out. Fold the corners, measure 1" down, and sew across. Tack the corners to the bottom of the bag.

3. Turn the bag right-side out.

4. Add a special button and a black tassel to the loop, as shown in the photo below.

Add a button and black tassel to the front for a stylish finish.

Sari
Saffron

The border of fabric taken from a sari brought back from India, combined with beaded tassels and a beaded handle, creates a one-of-a-kind festive bag.

finished size

8" x 7½"

fabric and notions

11" x 25" sari piece or ⅓-yard fabric

⅓-yard dupioni silk

9" x 25" piece fusible craft fleece

14" beaded fringe

Sewing thread to match fabric

Decorative thread

Decorative bead strap

Erasable pen

Pins

Scissors

Iron

Patterns

prepare

1. Cut, as follows:

- one sari fabric piece of pattern #FOUR-1* and save the scraps (bag body)
- one silk dupioni piece of pattern #FOUR-1* (lining)
- one fusible fleece piece of pattern #FOUR-1 (lining)
- 2" x 6" sari fabric piece from above saved scrap (loops)

*Make clips as designated on the pattern. Trim away the ½" seam allowance from the fleece.

2. Place the wrong side of the sari fabric on the fusible side of the fleece and press. Treat as one piece.

loops

1. Fold the 6" strip in half lengthwise with wrong sides together and press.

2. Bring the edges to meet the inside fold and press.

3. Topstitch close to the two folded edges.

4. Cut in half.

5. Fold each in half and pin to the right side of the sari fabric under the clip as shown on the pattern.

The hand-loomed sari designed with patterned borders is embellished with golden beaded fringe and a jeweled strap.

bead fringe

1. Mark the ½" seam line, with an erasable pen, along the curve of the flap.

2. Place the beginning of the beaded fringe along this line. The beaded fringe is attached to a tape that must be "eased" into the curve of the flap. If easing is not done, the flap will not lay flat, and it will "cup." Start and end the beaded fringe ½" inside from the side seams.

3. Face the beads toward the inside of the bag and baste in place by hand, as shown in Figure 4-55.

4. Place the sari fabric and the dupioni lining with right sides together and pin around the curve of the flap.

5. With the sari fabric facing up, sew the sari fabric and the dupioni silk together with a backstitch to secure the beads. Follow the previous basting stitches.

6. Make a few clips around the flap's curve, stopping short of clipping into the hand-sewn seam line.

Secure the bead fringe with a backstitch.

Figure 4-55

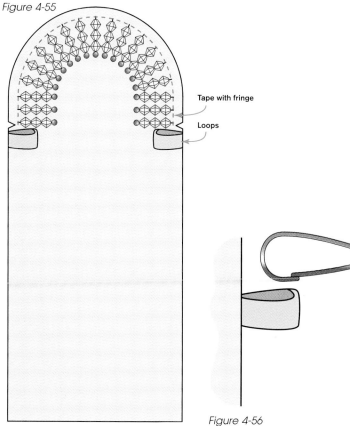

Tape with fringe

Loops

assemble

1. With the sari fabric and dupioni right sides together, sew the end opposite the curved flap with a ½" seam allowance. Trim seam to ¼".

2. Turn the bag right-side out and press.

3. Bring the straight end up to meet the beginning of the flap with right sides together. Pin the side seams and sew with a ½" seam allowance. Trim to ¼" and finish the raw edges by serging or with a zigzag stitch.

4. Turn the bag right-side out.

5. Add a snap hook to each loop and snap on a beaded strap, as shown in Figure 4-56.

Figure 4-56

Shades
of
Monet

This small purse with a circular handle converts into a clutch bag when folded over. The beautifully multicolor dyed fabric with asymmetrical pleating spoke for itself and did not need any embellishing except for the bamboo handles. It is lined with silk dupioni and quilted with meandering rayon thread. The ties are decorative and capture the circular handles.

finished size
10½" x 10"

fabric and notions

½-yard multicolored, pleated fabric

½-yard green silk dupioni

Air-Lite batting

2 4"-diameter circular bamboo handles

Spray adhesive

Sewing thread to match fabric

Decorative rayon thread

1 set magnetic snaps

Fasturn

Pins

Scissors

Patterns

prepare

1. Cut, as follows:
- two multicolored pleated fabric pieces of pattern #FIVE-1 (bag body)
- two silk dupioni pieces of pattern #FIVE-1 (lining)
- two batting pieces of pattern #FIVE-1 (lining)
- two 2" x 30" silk dupioni bias strips (ties)

2. Spray adhesive on the wrong side of the silk lining, place on the batting, and smooth down.

3. Stay-stitch around the circular curve ⅜" from the edge. Do this for all four pieces.

embellish

1. Thread the sewing machine with rayon thread.

2. Attach the free-motion foot.

3. Quilt each dupioni silk lining piece with a meandering stitch or use your favorite quilting design.

ties and snap

1. Fold the two long 30" strips in half lengthwise with right sides together.

2. Sew both strips with a ½" seam allowance.

3. Cut each strip into 4½" increments; 12 ties are needed.

4. Sew across one short end of each strip with a ½" seam allowance. Be sure to backstitch on the sewing machine when starting and stopping to keep the stitches from coming apart. Trim seam to ¼".

5. Turn each tube right-side out with a Fasturn.

6. Pin the tubes in pairs.

7. Place the pairs around the circular opening, as indicated on the pattern. Place three sets on each silk lining piece, as shown in Figure 4-57. One is positioned in the center of the curve with the raw edges of the ties aligning with the raw edge of the curve. The other two sets are placed ⅝" in from the top of the bag to allow a seam allowance for the bag's top. Use the same placements for the other side. Baste them in place.

8. Mark the position for the magnetic snap, as shown in Figure 4-58.

9. Cut the two small holes for the prongs on each side.

10. Send the prongs into the fabric and fold the prongs down toward the sides.

(continued)

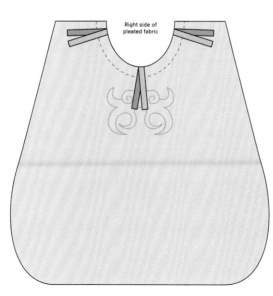

Figure 4-57

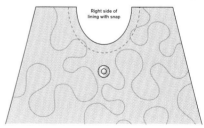

Figure 4-58

assemble

1. Place the two lining pieces with right sides together, pin, and sew the sides down around the bottom corner with a ½" seam allowance. Leave a 5" opening in the center of the bottom of the bag. Trim the seams to ¼". Clip around the curve up to the seam.

2. Place the two multicolored pieces with right sides together. Pin. Sew the side seams and bottom with a ½" seam allowance. Trim the seams to ¼" and clip curves.

3. Turn right-side out.

4. Place the multicolored bag inside the silk lining bag with right sides together, pin, and sew around the top and circular opening with a ½" seam allowance. Make sure the ties do not get in the way while sewing across the top. Trim seam to ¼" and clip the curve up to the seam.

5. Turn the bag right-side out through the opening.

6. Slipstitch the opening closed.

7. Tie the round bamboo handles in place with double-knots, as shown below.

It's not just a multicolored bag or clutch; reverse it for yet a third look.

Add handles by tying them to the bag body.

This purse can also be folded for use as a clutch, if you prefer.

Sunday
Best

This bag, the perfect accompaniment to carry to a wedding or Southern brunch, is the stuff of which Scarlet O'Hara's dreams were made. It is covered with lace and embellished with two Lucite® bangle bracelets used as handles. And, it's reversible!

finished size
10" x 8"

fabric and notions

½-yard lace

½-yard turquoise chiffon fabric

½-yard white-on-white leopard print cotton fabric

4 yards white rayon braid

Air-Lite batting

2 4"-diameter round clear plastic bracelets or handles

Sewing thread to match fabric

White thread

Clear polyester thread

Free-motion sewing machine foot

Spray adhesive

Pins

Scissors

Beaded closure

Measuring tape

Patterns

Bcaded pin (optional)

---

note

If you cannot find a large piece of lace, use wide strips of lace and just place them in rows next to each other or overlap them slightly. The lace will be quilted to the turquoise chiffon and batting with clear polyester thread using free-motion.

---

prepare

1. Spray adhesive on the wrong side of the turquoise chiffon, place on the batting, and smooth in place.

2. Cut, as follows:
- two turquoise chiffon-batting pieces of pattern #FIVE-1 (bag body)
- two white leopard print fabric pieces of pattern #FIVE-1 (lining)
- two lace pieces of pattern #FIVE-1 (body overlay)

3. Place the lace over the turquoise chiffon and center the lace design. If using wide strips, check the placement so no gaps occur. Pin in place and trim the lace to the purse shape, if necessary.

4. Stay-stitch around the circular opening ⅜" from the edge. Do the same for all four pieces.

embellish

1. Thread the sewing machine with clear polyester thread. Monofilament thread can also be used, but the polyester thread is easier to handle and can withstand a higher iron heat. Fill the bobbin with white thread.

2. Attach the free-motion foot. Lower the feed dogs.

3. Free-motion stitch over the lace by sewing along the lace patterns. Travel to another design by stitching along the fine lace threads. If you are joining wide lace strips, be sure to free-motion over those edges.

Add a decorative pin, if desired.

ties

1. Tie a knot at the beginning of the white rayon braid and pull to secure.

2. Measure 8" down and tie a knot there. Then, tie another knot next to the other and cut them apart in between. Do this until you have six braids with knots at each end.

3. Fold the braids in half and pin.

4. Place the braids around the circular opening. Place three sets on each white cotton lining piece, as shown in Figure 4-59. One set is placed in the center of the curve with the fold of the braid aligning with the raw edge of the curve. The other two sets are placed ⅝" in from the top of the bag to allow a seam allowance at the top of the bag. Use the same placements for the other side. Baste them in place.

Figure 4-59

Use the ties to attach the handles.

assemble

1. Place the two white cotton lining pieces with right sides together, pin, and sew the sides down around the bottom corner with a ½" seam allowance. Leave a 5" opening in the center of the bottom of the bag. Trim the seams to ¼". Clip around the curve up to the seam.

2. Place the lace-turquoise chiffon pieces with right sides together, pin, and sew the side seams and bottom with a ½" seam allowance. Trim the seams to ¼". Clip around the curves.

3. Turn right-side out.

4. Place the lace-turquoise chiffon bag inside the white cotton lining bag, right sides together.

5. Pin the top edges together and sew around the top and circular opening with a ½" seam allowance. Make sure the ties do not get in the way while sewing across the top. Trim to ¼" and clip the curve up to the seam.

6. Turn the bag right-side out through the opening.

7. Slipstitch closed.

8. Optional: Add a beaded pin, as shown below.

If the lace is a bit too much for your occasion, reverse the purse for a more casual look.

Heavy Date

This purse is made from the same pattern as the previous two bags, Shades of Monet and Sunday Best, but with a curved opening and no handles, so if necessary, refer back to them, pages 78 and 81, for illustrated assistance. Little loops were added into the side seam for clipping on a strap. Without the straps, it converts into a clutch bag. The fabric is embellished with zigzag stitches. On one side, the lines are satin stitched with green metallic thread, and on the other side, they are straight stitched with rayon thread. These decorative stitches also serve as the quilting to hold the layers together. The edge of the opening is adorned with sparkling bead fringe. ●

finished size
8" x 10"

fabric and notions

½-yard purple-and-green cotton print fabric

1 yard purple silk dupioni

Air-Lite batting

12" x 14" piece tear-away stabilizer

20" beaded fringe

2 12" x 14" sheets quilting paper

Sewing thread to match fabric

Decorative green metallic and purple rayon threads

10" x 6" plastic canvas

Zigzag or satin stitch foot

Spray adhesive

2 silver lanyards

Chalk or erasable pen

Fasturn

Pins

Scissors

Patterns

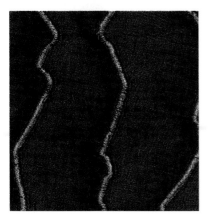

Use a zigzag stitch in a smooth and slow fashion to create this flap effect.

prepare

1. Cut, as follows:
- 10" x 6" plastic canvas piece following pattern #SIX-1 dotted lines
- two purple silk dupioni pieces of pattern #SIX-1* (bag body)
- two purple-and-green cotton print pieces of pattern #SIX-1* (lining)
- two batting pieces of pattern #SIX-1* (lining)
- 2" x 6" purple silk dupioni bias strip (loops)
- 2" x 48" purple silk dupioni bias strip (strap)

embellish

1. Select a quilting design or use the zigzag similar to the one shown in the project.
2. Make two copies tracing the shape of pattern #SIX-1 on quilting paper.
3. Place it over the quilting design and trace enough to fill the pattern shape. Place one sheet on each of the purple silk/batting pieces and pin in place.
4. Thread the machine with purple rayon thread and purple sewing thread in the bobbin.
5. Using a regular straight stitch foot, sew along the lines of the paper. Zigzag over the fabric with a smooth and slow machine stitch, to achieve the look shown in the accompanying photo at left.
6. When finished, tear the paper away.
7. Thread the machine with the green metallic thread and

2. Lightly spray adhesive on the wrong side of the purple silk, place on the batting, and smooth down.
3. Make marks, with a chalk or erasable pen, where the loops will be placed, according to the pattern placement.
*As a precaution, cut all the pieces 2" larger around the perimeter to allow for shrinkage with embellishment. Then they will have to be re-cut with the pattern before assembling.

matching green sewing thread in the bobbin.
8. Attach a zigzag or satin stitch foot.
9. Place the sheet of tear-away stabilizer under the batting and pin in place.
10. Using the same lines, satin stitch slowly following the zigzag lines. Start in the center and work your way to the sides.
11. Tear away the stabilizer.
12. Re-cut both pieces with pattern #SIX-1.

(continued)

note

Before attempting step 9, stitch a practice swatch on the same layers of fabric/batt. The back of the foot has an open channel to allow all the stitching to escape smoothly. Use a 3cm width, or test several widths and see which looks best.

beaded fringe

1. Mark the seam allowance across the tops of the purple silk pieces with chalk or an erasable pen.

2. Align the beginning of the bead fringe with the mark, as shown in Figure 4-60. The tape that holds the beaded fringe must be "eased on" and placed loosely. If not, the braid may cause the opening to pull and "cup." Baste in place. Do the same for the other side. Begin and end ½" in from the side seams.

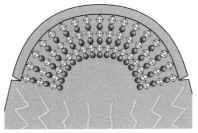

Figure 4-60

Ease on the beaded fringe tape so it lays flat.

loops and strap

1. Fold the strip in half lengthwise with right sides together. Sew with a ½" seam allowance and turn right-side out with a Fasturn.

2. Cut strip in half to 3" length.

3. Fold in half and pin.

4. Place where marked on the purple silk side seams and baste in place, as shown in Figure 4-61. Make sure the fold of the loops face the center of the bag.

Figure 4-61

5. Fold the long strip in half lengthwise with right sides together.

6. Sew with a ½" seam.

7. Turn right-side out with a Fasturn.

8. Tuck the raw edges at each tube end back into itself to clean finish the ends.

9. Thread each end through a silver clip, creating a ½" loop, and sew the ends to the strap.

assemble

1. Place the two purple silk pieces with right sides together, pin, and sew the side seams and bottom with a ½" seam allowance. Trim the seams to ¼" and clip the curves.

2. Turn right-side out.

3. Place the two purple and green cotton print pieces with right sides together. Sew side seams and bottom with a ½" seam allowance, leaving a 5" opening at the center of the bottom. Trim the seams to ¼" and clip the curves to the seam.

4. Place the purple silk bag inside the purple and green lining bag, right sides together. Align the top edges and pin together. Backstitch by hand over the basting stitches holding the beaded fringe.

5. Turn the bag right-side out through the 5" opening.

6. Roll the plastic canvas into a tube shape and send it through the

5" opening and maneuver it between the lining and the green satin stitched side.

7. Slipstitch the opening closed.

8. Snap the strap clips onto the side loops.

Plum and celadon beads, a shimmer of silk, and a swinging strap come together for a memorable evening.

Weekend in
Acapulco

This great turquoise beaded bag makes clever use of a beaded belt with a chain and snap closure as the strap. Since the belt just snaps on, it can be taken off and still be used as a belt accessory. All these ingenious tricks are just the thing for packing light while traveling. The silk fabric used to create the bag is embellished with lustrous rayon threads and was beaded by hand with tiny, round beads. Keep several handles ready for this bag—or just tuck the end loops inside the bag and use it as a clutch.

finished size
5½" x 11"

fabric and notions

1 yard turquoise dupioni silk

Fusible craft fleece

2 2" squares fusible interfacing

Plastic canvas:
- 2 11" x 4½" pieces
- 2" x 11" piece

2 12" x 14" sheets quilting paper

Sewing thread to match fabric

Decorative rayon, metallic, or polyester embroidery thread

Beads with holes large enough for a needle to pass through

1 set magnetic snaps

Chalk marker

Fabri-Tac

23mm silver lanyard (if the belt has a silver chain)

Beading needle

Pins

Scissors

Patterns

Polyester clear thread (optional)

notes

○This bag is lined with the same fabric as the exterior.

○Use chalk for marking, as it will not be affected by heat. If an erasable marker is used and set with heat, it may become permanent.

prepare

1. Cut, as follows:
- two turquoise dupioni silk pieces of pattern #SEVEN-1 (body and lining)
- one fusible fleece piece of pattern #SEVEN-1 (lining)
- two turquoise dupioni silk pieces of pattern #SEVEN-2 (flap)
- one fusible fleece piece of pattern #SEVEN-2 (flap)
- two 2" x 6" turquoise dupioni silk strips (loops)
- three plastic canvas shapes as provided on the pattern (two 11" x 4½" pieces and one 2" x 11" piece)

embellish

1. Trace the design for the body of the bag onto the quilting paper.
2. Place the paper over the silk/fleece piece and pin in place.
3. Thread the sewing machine with decorative thread. Use the appropriate needle. Set up for free-motion.
4. Quilt, as shown in Figure 4-62, through all layers following the lines for the design. When finished, tear the paper away.

Figure 4-62

2. Trim away the seam allowances around the perimeter of the square of fleece cut from pattern # SEVEN-1.
3. Place the wrong side of the dupioni on the fusible side of the fleece and press with a Teflon pressing sheet.
4. Trim away the seam allowance on the fleece for the flap.
5. Place the wrong side of the silk flap on the fusible side of the fleece. Press.
6. Mark the magnetic snap placement on the remaining silk piece with chalk. This will be the lining.
7. Center the fusible interfacing on the wrong side of the silk where the magnetic snap will be placed.

5. Do the same for the flap silk/fleece piece, as in Figure 4-63.

Figure 4-63

6. Select one side of the rectangle piece to be the front. If unsure, refer to the pattern to see where the tops and sides are located on the rectangle. You will be hand-beading the front and the front flap only. Do not bead the back of the bag, as it will press on your body and may loosen the beads.

(continued)

7. Thread a beading needle with turquoise sewing thread in a single strand, tying a knot at the end.

8. Begin beading at the center of the bag front. Start the needle from the back and bring it out to the front at the end of a curl and then sew through a bead going back down close to the edge of the bead. Sew through the bead once more and then send your needle over to the next curl.

9. Repeat the process, but after sewing several beads, tie a knot in the back for security. If your beads are larger, you may want to consider knotting after each bead. Do not bead near the seam areas.

10. Bead the flap in the same manner.

Bead the front of the bag by hand with a single strand of sewing thread, knotting after several beads.

loops

1. Fold the 6" long strip of silk in half lengthwise with right sides together and sew with a ½" seam allowance.

2. Turn right-side out with a Fasturn.

3. Cut into two 3" lengths.

4. Fold in half and place one on each side seam on the right side of the bag. The raw edges of the loop are aligned with the opening of the bag, as shown in Figure 4-62 on previous page.

assemble

1. Fold the embellished square in half. Sew with a ½" seam allowance and press seams open. Fold the corners, measure down 1", and sew across. Face the points toward the center and tack down. Turn right-side out.

2. Fold the silk for the lining in half and sew sides with a ½" seam allowance. Press seams open. Fold the corners, measure down 1" and sew across.

3. Place the embellished flap and the lining with right sides together, as shown in Figure 4-64. Sew with a ½" seam around the curve only. Sew another line of stitching close to the previous one in the seam allowance. Trim the seam allowance to ¼". Clip the curve up to the seam line. Make the clips ½" apart.

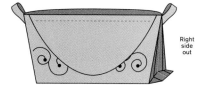

Figure 4-64

4. Turn right-side out.

5. Pin the two straight edges together. Center the flap along the back of the embellished bag with right sides together, pin, and sew with a ½" seam allowance.

6. Place the embellished bag (with loops and flap) inside the lining bag with right sides together, as shown in Figure 4-65. Bring the top edges together and pin.

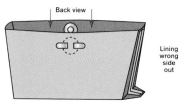

Figure 4-65

7. Sew with a ½" seam allowance, leaving a 6" opening in the center back. Trim seam to ¼".

8. Turn the bag right-side out through the opening, as shown in Figure 4-66.

Figure 4-66

9. Roll up one of the plastic canvas pieces. Notice that these pieces are shaped like a wide "V." The wider side is the top. Roll from one short end to the other end. Place it inside the front of the bag between the batting and the lining. Let it unroll and open flat. Push it around until it creates an even shape in the bag. Run a thin bead of glue between the batting and the plastic canvas, making sure it does not soak through the fleece. Do the same for the back of the bag.

10. Place the small rectangle of plastic canvas in the bottom of the bag. Again, run a small bead of glue between the fleece and the plastic canvas. The glue sets slowly, so there is time to slide the plastic canvas around until it is positioned evenly in the bag.

11. Slipstitch the opening closed.

12. Place a lanyard on one of the loops. Clip the lanyard onto the chain portion of the belt. Clip the lanyard that is on the belt to the other loop, as shown in the accompanying photo.

Clip the lanyard in place to form the finished strap.

Starlet

This elegant bag with black-and-white feather fringe is just the right accessory for a gala evening affair. The feathers are accented with black brocade. Where will you be when the paparazzi arrive?

finished size

11" x 5"

fabric and notions

1 yard white-on-white print cotton fabric

Fusible craft fleece

1 yard black brocade

Air-Lite batting

18" feather fringe

1 yard 1"-diameter round cotton cord

White and black sewing thread

18" polyester boning

Pins

Scissors

Patterns

note

The feather fringe is approximately 6" long.

prepare

1. Cut, as follows:

- four white-on-white print cotton fabric pieces of pattern #EIGHT-1 (bag body)
- two fusible fleece pieces of pattern #EIGHT-1 (lining)
- 5" x 17" black brocade bias strip (trim)
- 2½" x 16" black brocade bias strip (handle)
- 2½" x 7" black brocade bias strip (front loop)
- 16" length cotton cord (handle)
- 7" length cotton cord (front loop)

2. Trim the ½" seam allowance from the perimeter of the craft fleece piece. Do not trim away the seam allowance from the darts. The thickness of the fleece at the darts will help keep the shape at the bottom of the bag.

3. Place the wrong side of the white cotton piece on the fusible side of the fleece. Do the same with the other fleece. Press to adhere.

assemble

1. Referring to Figure 4-67, pin and sew the two darts on each of the four pieces with a ¼" seam. Press the darts toward the center.

2. Place the two white cotton-fleece pieces with right sides together, pin, and sew the sides and bottom with a ½" seam allowance. Trim the seams to ¼". Clip the curves up to the seam.

3. Turn right-side out.

4. Repeat steps 2 and 3 for the remaining two white cotton pieces.

5. Place other bag inside the one turned right-side out, as in Figure 4-68. Match the side seams, pin together around the opening, and baste.

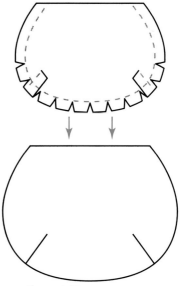

Figure 4-68

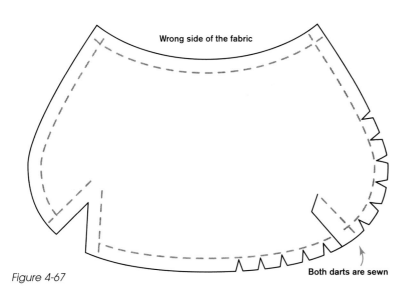

Figure 4-67

Wrong side of the fabric

Both darts are sewn

handle and front loop

1. Fold the 16" strip of black brocade in half lengthwise with right sides together. Sew with a ½" seam allowance.

2. Turn right-side out with a Fasturn while filling it with the cotton cord.

3. Pull the edge of the brocade tube back and cut off 1" of the cord, then slip the cord inside the tube. Do the same for the other end.

4. Fold the round tube into a loop and place the ends side by side. Baste together, trying to place the seam on the inside of the loop.

5. Fold the 7" strip of black brocade in half lengthwise with right sides together. Sew with a ½" seam allowance.

6. Repeat steps 2 through 4 on the 7" front loop strip.

Once attached to the bag body, the handle and front loop come together for a handy closure.

feather fringe

1. Place a pin in the center of the front and back of the bag. (They are the same, so just designate one side as the front and one as the back.)

2. Place the fringe along the top edge of the bag, starting at the center of the back and pin the fringe all the way around and overlap the ends at least an inch where they join.

3. Baste in place through the fabric binding at the top of the fringe.

note

Before sewing the bias trim, test the front and back loops. Pull the back loop through the front loophole and pull up until the top of the front loop rests behind the loop handle. If the front loop is too loose, shorten the length now. The loops may vary due to the difference in cotton cords or the weave of the brocade.

trim

1. Place the ends of the loop handle in the center of the back over the feathers. The edges should align with the top of the bag. Baste in place.

2. Place the ends of the front loop in the center of the front over the feathers. The edges should align with the top of the bag. Baste in place.

3. Fold the long 17" bias strip of black brocade in half, placing the short ends with right sides together. Sew with a ½" seam allowance. Trim seam to ¼" and press the seam open.

4. Fold the bias strip of black brocade in half lengthwise with wrong sides together and press. Sew along the raw edges with a ¼" seam allowance.

5. Place the folded bias strip around the opening of the bag over the feathers and with the joining seam at the center of the back, as

shown in Figure 4-69. The raw edges of the bias strip should align with the top edge of the bag. Pin in place.

(continued)

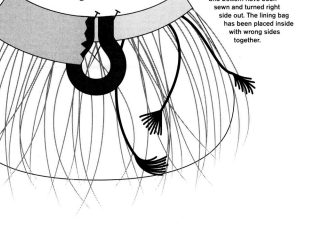

Figure 4-69

Right side of fabric sides and bottom have been sewn and turned right side out. The lining bag has been placed inside with wrong sides together.

finish

1. Stitch around the top of the bag with a ½" seam (which should be where the fabric binding ends) at the edge through all layers of bag, feather fringe, black brocade bias, the front loop, and the handle, as shown in Figure 4-70 (front view) and Figure 4-71 (back). If it is difficult to sew on the machine, sew the seam by hand. Use a backstitch to secure.

2. The bias strip will be folded over the seam allowances and stitched down on the inside, creating the layers illustrated in Figure 4-72, but first, place the polyester boning inside the bias strip fold around the top of the bag and pin it in place. This boning helps to keep the shape of the opening.

3. Place the strip of batting over the polyester boning. This will pad the black brocade trim to match the handle loops.

4. Place the bias strip carefully over the batting, boning, and seam allowances to the inside of the bag. Pull it taut, trying to keep the rounded shape of the trim the same size as the loops. Pin the edge down and then slipstitch in place.

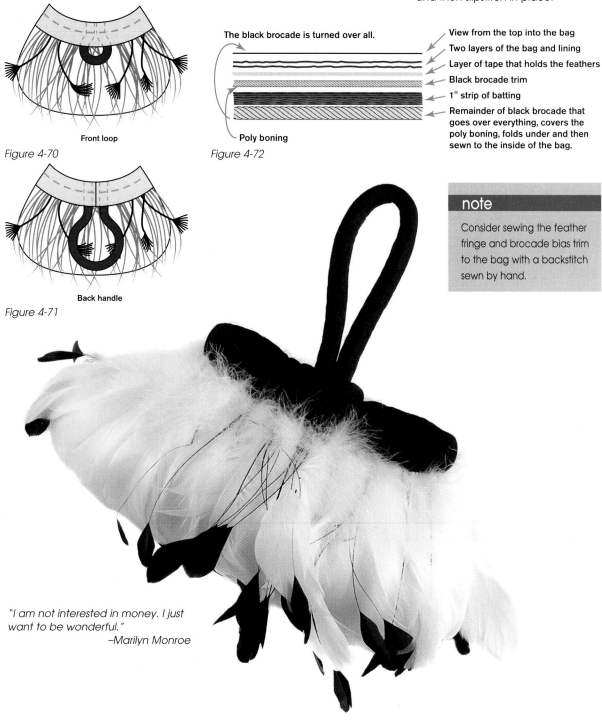

Front loop

Figure 4-70

Back handle

Figure 4-71

The black brocade is turned over all.

Poly boning

Figure 4-72

View from the top into the bag
Two layers of the bag and lining
Layer of tape that holds the feathers
Black brocade trim
1" strip of batting
Remainder of black brocade that goes over everything, covers the poly boning, folds under and then sewn to the inside of the bag.

note

Consider sewing the feather fringe and brocade bias trim to the bag with a backstitch sewn by hand.

"I am not interested in money. I just want to be wonderful."
–Marilyn Monroe

Shibori Purse

A very special kimono made from shibori was taken apart and some of the fabric was used to create this purse. The simple lines of this purse allow the beauty of the vintage fabric to take center stage. A zippered opening allows for easy access and the handle attached with lanyards allows you to change the handles. For an evening out, add a handle made with beads.

finished size

6" x 9"

fabric and notions

½-yard shibori fabric

¼-yard lavender silk dupioni

Air-Lite batting

9" polyester boning

Spray adhesive

2 lanyards

16" zipper

Fasturn

Sewing thread

Zipper foot

Zigzag foot

Pins

Scissors

Patterns

> **note**
>
> Shibori is a traditional textile art dating back to the eighth century. The word shibori comes from the root word "shiboru" which means to wring or squeeze. The cloth is sewn, bound, and gathered by hand to create a design and then dyed. An apprentice studies for 13 years and sometimes a kimono may take a year to complete.

prepare

1. Cut, as follows:
- two shibori fabric pieces of pattern #NINE-1 (bag body)
- two lavender silk dupioni pieces of pattern #NINE-1 (lining)
- two batting pieces of pattern #NINE-1 (lining)
- two 2" x 3" shibori strips (loops)
- 2" x 11" shibori bias strips (handle)

2. Spray the wrong side of the shibori fabric, place on the batting, and smooth down.

3. Fold the 2" x 3" shibori strips in half with right sides together.

4. When folded, sew the strips with a ½" seam allowance.

> **note**
>
> Place the pattern on the shibori to capture a specific part of the design. Just remember that the narrow end is the top of the bag and the wider end is the bottom of the bag.

5. Turn right-side out.

6. Fold in half and pin.

7. Before assembly of the bag, the wrong side of the silk lining should be placed on the batting and quilted. Do both pieces.

assemble

1. Place one shibori piece with a silk lining with right sides together. Sew across the top with a ½" seam allowance. Trim the batting from the seam allowance and press open. Do the same for the other shibori-batting and silk lining piece.

2. Place these two pieces with right sides together. Make sure the shibori pieces are touching each other and the silk-batting linings as well. Line up the center seams of both pieces and pin in place.

3. Stitch-in-the-ditch 3" from each end. Backstitch to secure.

4. Fold the fabrics so that the shibori/batting pieces and the lining are with wrong sides together with a finished opening. Press the seam.

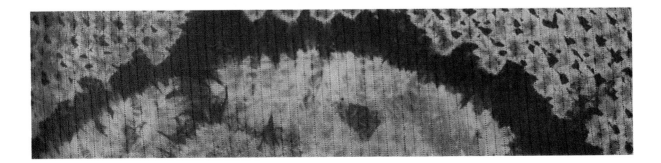

zipper

1. Referring to Figure 4-73, place the zipper under the opening at the center of the bag with the opening edge around the teeth of the zipper. Pin in place.

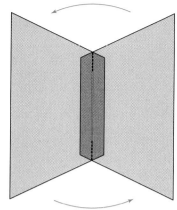

Figure 4-73

2. Place the zipper foot on the sewing machine and make the needed adjustments. Sew close to the edge of the opening around the zipper and then cut the excess zipper away.
3. Fold the bag in half with the shibori sides together and pin the sides.

4. Place the loops inside the bag at the top of the fold. Place the loop ends inside the seam allowance and sew with a ½" seam allowance, as shown in Figure 4-74. Trim the seam to ½". Finish the edges with a zigzag stitch.

Figure 4-74

5. Unzip the zipper. Sew across the bottom of the bag with a ½" seam allowance. Trim the seam to ½" and finish the edge with a zigzag stitch, as shown in Figure 4-75.

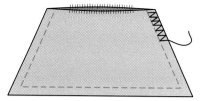

Unzip zipper and leave open.
Sew around the sides and bottom.
Trim seams and finish with zigzag.

Figure 4-75

6. Fold the corners of the bottom of the bag, measure 1" down, and sew across. Face the points of the corners toward the center of the bag and tack in place.
7. Turn the bag right-side out through the unzipped opening.

Zipper is done.

handle

1. Fold the 10" strip of shibori in half lengthwise with right sides together and sew with a ½" seam allowance, as shown in Figure 4-75.

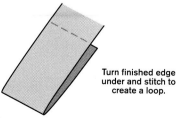

Sew seam and turn right-side out.

Figure 4-75

5. Fold the ends over a scant ½" (creating a loop at the end of the handle, as in Figure 4-78) and sew the edge to the handle. Do the same for the other side.

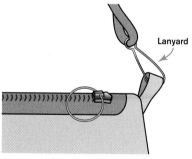

Turn finished edge under and stitch to create a loop.

Figure 4-78

2. Turn right-side out with a Fasturn.
3. Slide the boning through the fabric tube, as in Figure 4-76.

Slide boring into tube.

Figure 4-76

6. Place a lanyard through each loop, pull the handle loop to the small end of the lanyard, and clip the lanyard through the loops at each end of the zippered top, as in Figure 4-79.

4. Turn the raw edges of the tube inside the tube ½" on both sides, as shown in Figure 4-77.

Turn raw edge under.

Figure 4-77

Lanyard

Figure 4-79

Cochin
Clutch

All eyes will be on you when you make your entrance with this purse. The elegant black feathers with a turquoise sheen wrap a small pouch made of hand-dyed vintage silk. The top of the bag is trimmed with black brocade and a clasp is fashioned from a turquoise pendant and tasseled braid.

finished size
6½" x 7"

fabric and notions

½-yard hand-dyed black silk

⅛-yard black brocade

Air-Lite batting

1⅔ yards black braid

16" black feather fringe

3 black tassels

Pendant or pin

Thread to match fabric

Spray adhesive

Measuring tape

Iron

Pins

Scissors

Patterns

note
The feather fringe is approximately 9" long.

prepare

1. Cut, as follows:
- four hand-dyed black silk pieces of pattern #TEN-1, including the white notches (body)
- two batting pieces of pattern #TEN-1 (lining)
- 2½" x 15" black brocade bias strip (trim)
- 50" black braid piece (strap)
- 6" black braid piece (closure)

assemble

1. Spray the two pieces of batting with adhesive. Place a piece of silk over each with the right sides facing up. Smooth in place.

3. Turn the bag right-side out.

2. Place two silk-batting pieces with right sides together. Sew the sides and bottom with a ½" seam allowance. Trim to a ¼" seam allowance and clip the curves up to the seam.

4. Place the remaining two pieces of silk-batting with right sides together and sew the sides and bottom with a ½" seam allowance. Trim to a ¼" seam allowance and clip the curves up to the seam.

5. Place one silk-batting bag inside the other with wrong sides together, as shown in Figure 4-80.

6. Align the top edges of the two bags and pin. Create pleats at the top of the bag. Bring the white notches together, with the pleats facing the center of the bag. Baste in place, as shown in Figure 4-81.

Lining

Hand dyed fabric backed with batting.

Seams sewn and turned right side out.

Figure 4-80

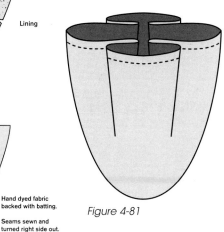

Figure 4-81

embellish

1. Starting at the center back, place the feather fringe around the top edge of the bag. Go around the opening of the bag, returning to the center of the back. There should be an overlap at the center back. Pin the fringe in place through the tape that holds the feathers.

2. Pin one strap end at each side seam over the tape that holds the feather fringe, as shown in Figure 4-82.

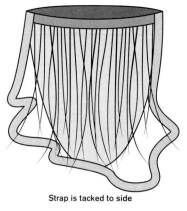

Strap is tacked to side

Figure 4-82

closure loop

1. Positioning the tassel loops as shown in Figure 4-83, place a tassel on the 6" braid and push it to the center, as in Figure 4-84.

2. Bring the two ends of the braid together to create a loop.

3. Pin the tasseled loop in place at the center back over the feather fringe. Make the loop smaller or use as is, depending on your closure.

Braid

Figure 4-83

Figure 4-84

finish

1. Fold the 2½"-wide strip in half, bringing the two short ends with right sides together. (Depending on the thickness of the binding that holds the feathers, this bias trim may have to be longer or shorter.) Sew with a ½" seam allowance. Press the seam open.

2. Place the strip around the top of the bag with the right side of the brocade against the feather fringe binding, as shown in Figure 4-85, and pin in place. Make sure to line up the seam in the trim with one of the side seams of the bag.

3. Sew around the top edge with a ½" seam allowance (or more because of the bulk of the feather fringe tape). If it is too difficult to sew through all the layers with the sewing machine, sew by hand with a backstitch. Finger-press the strip up.

4. Fold the trim over the seam allowances and feather binding. Fold the trim edge under approximately ½" and bring the folded edge of the trim to the seam line on the inside of the bag, as shown in Figure 4-86. Sew by hand with a blind stitch to finish.

Figure 4-85

Back

Figure 4-86

5. Place the pendant or pin in the center front of the bag on the black brocade trim, as shown in Figure 4-87.

Figure 4-87

Place a pendant or pin in the center front of the bag and bring tassel/loop over for the closure.

6. To close, bring the tasseled loop over and hook under the pendant or pin, as in Figure 4-88.

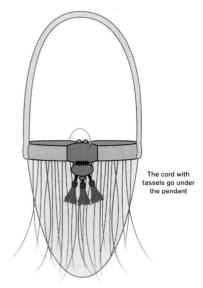

The cord with tassels go under the pendant

Figure 4-88

Don't forget:
✓Opening night tickets
✓Dangerously red lipstick.

Flower
Girl

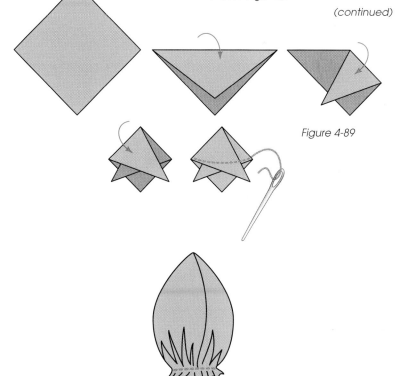

The silk baby roses and organza leaves capture a moment in time. This is a perfect little purse for a spring party or the flower girl and bridesmaids at a wedding. The sheerness of the fabric allows you to see the contents of the bag. Fill it with petals or wrap your lipstick in a beautiful heirloom hankie to place inside.

finished size

6½" x 6"

fabric and notions

1 yard sparkle organza

¼-yard muslin

10 1"-wide silk baby roses

Newspaper

Fabri-Tac

Sewing thread to match fabric

Fasturn

Pins

Scissors

Patterns

note

Consider adding rhinestones, crystals, or pearls between the flowers and leaves. For a summer look, use a variety of silk flowers or daisies and sprigs of silk leaves.

prepare

1. Cut, as follows:

- two sparkle organza pieces of pattern #TEN-1, including the black notches (body)
- 3" x 11" sparkle organza piece (trim)
- two 2" x 17" sparkle organza pieces (straps)
- six 4" sparkle organza squares (leaves)
- 8" x 12" muslin piece

2. Referring to Figure 4-89, fold one 4" square in half with wrong sides together, from point to point. Bring one side point past the center. Bring the other side point past the center and pin both in place. By hand, sew a curved running stitch across the bottom.

3. Pull the thread to gather the curved bottom of the leaf, as shown in Figure 4-90. Gather to approximately ¾". Trim away the excess organza.

(continued)

Figure 4-89

Under side of the leaf   *Figure 4-90*

embellish

1. Cover your workspace with some newspaper and place the piece of muslin on the newspaper. While applying the glued roses, some of the glue will seep through the organza and onto the muslin. Do not move the organza until you are finished. Work quickly, apply the roses and leaves, then pull away the muslin and place the piece upside-down to dry. Let it dry overnight.

2. Position one of the organza body pieces on the muslin, right side up. Look at the flower and leaf placement shown in Figure 4-91 or the accompanying photo at far right. Arrange them on the organza and see if you would like to add more flowers or leaves.

3. Pin the leaves in place.

4. Remove one flower at a time, spread glue over the bottom, and replace the flower.

5. Unpin the leaf and place glue on the front and back of the bottom of the leaf and then replace the leaf. The glue will stay tacky long enough to move the leaves under the flowers so the raw edges do not show. The glue dries clear; place some glue on the side of the flowers so that the flowers are glued to each other as well as the organza.

6. When satisfied with the design, pull the muslin away and turn the organza upside-down, resting on the tips of the flowers.

Figure 4-91

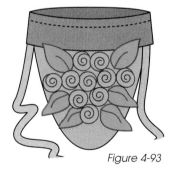

Arrange the flowers and leaves in the manner similar to that shown, or in alternate manner that exemplifies your own personal taste.

straps

1. Fold one of the strips lengthwise with right sides together.

2. Sew with a ½" seam along the length and then across one of the ends. Do the same for the other strip.

3. Turn right-side out using the Fasturn. Do not trim away the seam allowances.

assemble

1. Place the two body pieces with right sides together. Sew around the perimeter with a ½" seam allowance. Sew another seam alongside the first in the seam allowance. Trim, leaving a seam allowance of ¼".

2. Turn the body piece right-side out.

3. Create pleats at the top of the bag.

4. Bring the black notches together, with the pleats facing the center of the bag.

5. Pin one strap at each side seam, as shown in Figure 4-92. The raw edges of the strap should align with the top edge of the opening.

6. Fold the 3"-wide strip in half, bringing the two short ends with right sides together. Sew with a ½" seam allowance. Finger-press the seam open.

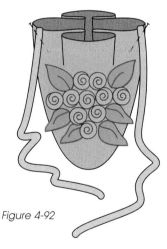

Figure 4-92

7. Fold the strip in half with wrong sides together and pin.

8. Place the strip around the top of the bag and pin in place. Make sure to line up the seam in the trim with one of the side seams of the bag.

9. Sew around the top edge with a ½" seam allowance, as shown in Figure 4-93. Finger-press the strip up.

Figure 4-93

10. Fold over the seam allowances and bring the folded edge of the trim to the seam line on the inside of the bag, as in Figure 4-94. Stitch-in-the-ditch or sew by hand with a blind stitch to finish.

Zanzibar

This stylish bag is a perfect addition to any wardrobe. It has a small flap and a hidden magnetic snap for security as well as decoration. It is lined with a matching green silk dupioni, which is quilted with black rayon thread. The bag is crowned with a black bead handle.

finished size

6½" x 11"

fabric and notions

⅓-yard monkey tapestry

¾-yard green silk dupioni

Fusible craft fleece

Iron-on tricot stabilizer

Sewing thread to match fabric

Decorative black rayon thread

1 set magnetic snaps

6" curved bead handle

Free-motion foot

Mini iron

Pins

Scissors

Patterns

prepare

1. Cut, as follows:
   - two monkey tapestry pieces of pattern #EIGHT-1 (bag body)
   - two green silk dupioni pieces of pattern #EIGHT-1 (lining)
   - two fusible fleece pieces of pattern #EIGHT-1 (lining)
   - one monkey tapestry piece of pattern #EIGHT-2 (flap)
   - one green silk dupioni piece of pattern #EIGHT-2 (flap)
   - one fusible fleece piece of pattern #EIGHT-2 (flap)
   - 4" x 16" green silk dupioni bias strip (trim)
   - 2" x 6" green silk dupioni bias strip (loops)
   - two 3" iron-on stabilizer squares (flap)

2. Trim the ½" seam allowance from perimeter of the lining fleece piece. Do not trim away the seam allowance from the darts. The thickness of the fleece at the darts will help to keep the shape at the bottom of the bag.

3. Place the wrong side of a green silk dupioni lining piece on the fusible side of the fleece lining. Do the same for the other piece.

4. Place the wrong side of the green silk dupioni flap on the fusible side of the fleece flap piece.

5. Mark the placement for the magnetic snap. One of the marks goes on the right side of the tapestry piece that is to be used as the front. The other mark goes on the right side of the silk dupioni flap lining.

6. Press a square of iron-on stabilizer on the wrong side of the tapestry fabric to reinforce the area where the snap will be applied.

7. Apply the magnetic snap by cutting two small slits and sending the prongs through. Bend the prongs to the side to anchor.

note

Use the mini iron to reach into small areas.

embellish

1. Thread the machine with black rayon thread and matching black sewing thread in the bobbin.

2. Put on the free-motion foot and quilt with a meandering design or with your favorite quilt design to embellish the green silk dupioni lining.

assemble

1. Sew the two darts on each of the tapestry pieces with a ¼" seam. Press the seam toward the center.

2. Place the two tapestry pieces with right sides together. Sew the sides and bottom with a ½" seam. Sew another seam right next to the first seam (within the seam allowance) to secure this loosely woven textile. Do not trim the seam. Clip the curve up to the seam.

3. Turn right-side out.

4. Sew the two darts on each of the quilted silk dupioni pieces with a ¼" seam. Press the seams toward the center.

5. Place the two quilted silk dupioni pieces with right sides together. Sew around the sides and bottom with a ½" seam allowance. Trim the seams to ¼" and clip the curves.

6. Place the silk dupioni lining inside the tapestry bag with wrong sides together, as shown in Figure 4-95. Match the side seams. Bring the top edges together and pin.

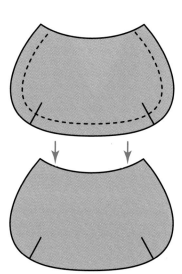

Figure 4-95

flap

1. Place the tapestry flap piece and the silk dupioni flap piece with right sides together. Pin and sew around the sides and the curved front edge with a ½" seam allowance.

2. Sew again right next to the seam (within the seam allowance). Trim the seam allowance to ¼" and clip the curves to the seam.

3. Turn right-side out and press.

4. Place the flap in the center of the back of the bag, upside-down with the tapestry fabrics right sides together. Baste in place.

loops

1. Fold the silk dupioni 6" strip in half lengthwise with right sides together. Pin and sew with a ½" seam allowance.

2. Turn right-side out with the Fasturn.

3. Press the seam to the side.

4. Cut in half.

5. Fold each piece in half and pin to the side seams on the tapestry fabric, so the silk dupioni loop edges are aligned with the top edge of the bag.

trim

1. Measure the opening of the bag at the seam line and add 1". Cut the 16" bias strip to that length.

2. Fold the silk dupioni 16" bias strip with right sides together. Pin and sew the short ends with a ½" seam allowance. Trim to ¼" and press the seams open.

3. Fold the strip in half with wrong sides together. Press.

4. Place the bias strip around the top of the bag, aligning the raw edges of the strip with the top of the bag. Pin and sew with a ½" seam allowance.

5. Fold the bias strip up and over the seam allowance's raw edges, as shown in Figure 4-96. Bring the folded edge of the bias strip to the inside of the bag and to the stitching line.

6. Slipstitch in place or stitch-in-the-ditch for the finished look shown in Figure 4-97.

(continued)

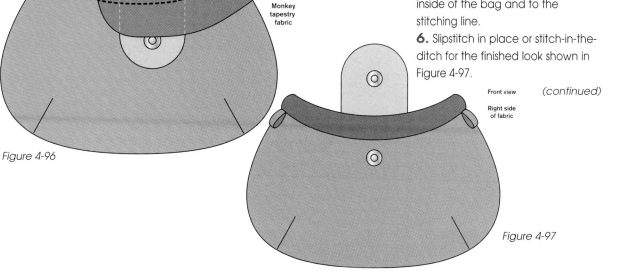

Loop

Back view
right side of fabric

Monkey
tapestry
fabric

Figure 4-96

Front view

Right side
of fabric

Figure 4-97

Attach the U-shaped handle to the loops on the bag's body.

handle

1. Remove the screw from the handle on each side.

2. Place the U-shaped hardware through the loop on each side of the bag.

3. Replace the handle in the top of the hardware and place the screw back through the hardware and handle. Screw in tightly on both sides.

Remember that fabulous dream you had of wandering the nature trails of the Jozani Forest of Zanzibar where the rare monkeys watched you from their leafy perches? This purse turns it into reality.

All That Jazz

This chic tote, with Ultrasuede with quilting that mimics the cut shape of the croc leather, is a perfect size for travel—or a midnight rendezvous at the local hot spot. The gleam from the elegant ebony faux bamboo handles balance the look of the embossed leather.

finished size
12" x 16"

fabric and notions

½-yard green Ultrasuede

½-yard green silk dupioni silk

2 17" x 5" pieces embossed crocodile leather

Fusible craft fleece

Air-Lite batting

4 sheets quilting paper

Sewing thread, green

Decorative rayon 30-weight threads, green and black

Fabri-Tac

2 black faux bamboo handles with hardware

Leather needle

#100 sharp sewing machine needle*

Pins

Scissors

Patterns

*Or choose a size and type that pierces the Ultrasuede without breaking the thread. This will vary with machines, so be sure to run a test sample.

prepare

1. Cut, as follows:
- two green Ultrasuede pieces of pattern #ELEVEN-1 (bag body)
- two green dupioni silk pieces of pattern #ELEVEN-1 (lining)
- two fleece pieces of pattern #ELEVEN-1 (lining)
- two batting pieces of pattern #ELEVEN-1 (lining)
- two embossed croc leather pieces of pattern #ELEVEN-2 (embellishment)
- ¾" x 12" green Ultrasuede piece (loops)

2. Cut the seam allowances away from the fleece and batting pieces.

3. Spray adhesive on the wrong side of the green silk pieces, place on the batting pieces, and smooth down.

embellish

1. Thread the sewing machine with 30-weight green rayon thread. Fill the bobbin with matching sewing thread.

2. Attach your free-motion foot and set up the machine for free-motion sewing.

3. Sew through the quilting paper, while following the lines.

4. When finished, tear off all the quilting paper.

5. Run a small bead of glue across the middle of the cutout leather strip. Place it at the bottom of the green Ultrasuede pieces. Press with your fingers and give it a few minutes to adhere.

4. Place the wrong sides of the green Ultrasuede down on the fusible side of the fleece pieces. Press to adhere. If the Ultrasuede does not adhere, use spray adhesive on the fleece. Test a small piece and spray lightly to see if the Ultrasuede is affected.

5. Trace the shape of the quilting design onto four sheets of quilting paper. Place one of each of the sheets on the Ultrasuede and silk dupioni. Pin in place.

Attach the crocodile leather to the Ultrasuede bag with one of two options detailed in step 4.

6. Thread the sewing machine with 30-weight black rayon thread. Fill the bobbin with matching sewing thread and use a leather needle.

7. Either use Option A or B next.

   A. Attach the free-motion foot and set up the machine for free-motion sewing. Be sure to lower the feed dogs. Carefully and slowly, sew along the cutout edge of the leather, as shown in Figure 4-98. Create a slightly longer sewing stitch while holding the fabric "taut." Do this by holding the fabric in front and back of the stitching area. If it still sticks, try covering the leather with a sheet of quilting paper. You can still see and feel the shape of the leather underneath. Remove the paper when finished.

Figure 4-98

B. Attach a Teflon foot or walking foot and set to a longer stitch length. Make sure your feed dogs are in the "up" position. Topstitch close to the cut edge, as in Figure 4-98.

loops

1. Cut the 12" strip of green Ultrasuede into 3" increments.
2. Fold each in half and pin. Place a pin in the center at the top of the quilted silk lining pieces.
3. Measure the width of the handles and divide by two. Place

finish

1. Place the Ultrasuede bag inside the lining bag with right sides together, as shown in Figure 4-100.
2. Pin the two top edges together and sew with a ½" seam allowance. Trim the seam to ¼".
3. Clip around the curve of the top.
4. Turn the bag right-side out through the bottom of the lining, as shown in Figure 4-101.
5. Thread the sewing machine with 30-weight rayon thread with matching rayon thread in the bobbin. Using a topstitch needle, topstitch around the finished edge of the bag ½" in from the edge.

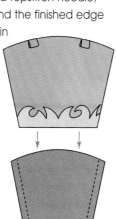

Figure 4-100

assemble

1. Place the two Ultrasuede pieces with right sides together, pin, and sew the side seams with a ½" seam allowance. Press the seams open. Sew the bottom with a ½" seam allowance and press seams open.
2. Fold the corner, measure down 2", and sew across.
3. Turn right-side out.

pins for that measurement in either direction out from the center pins. Remove the center pins.
4. Baste the loops in place. The edges of the loops should align with the top edge of the bag, as shown in Figure 4-99.

4. Place the two quilted silk lining pieces with right sides together. Sew the side seams with a ½" seam allowance. Press the seams open. Sew the bottom with a ½" seam allowance, leaving a 6" opening in the center.
5. Fold the corners, measure down 2" and sew across.

Figure 4-99

5. Place the handle over the loops to make sure the placement is accurate.

Lining

Figure 4-101

Slick ebony handles, elegant Ultrasuede, and faux croc leather equal haute design.

St. Moritz
Ski Trip

This luxurious bag is great for everyone who loves fur. The exquisite coloring of this faux fur is enhanced by using the fabric upside-down and allowing the fur tips to fall forward. The quick one-piece pattern turned this tote into a work of art in short order. I used metallic gold leather to create the trim as well as the handles. The handles were filled with a plastic hose from the hardware store to keep their shape and provide durability.

finished size

16" x 18"

fabric and notions

1 yard faux fur

1 yard cotton lining

Fusible craft fleece

Leather

2 16" lengths polyethylene ¼" tubing

6" zipper

Several clothespins or paperclips

Leather needle

Ballpoint needle

Sewing thread to match fur

Topstitch thread to match leather

Iron

Pins

Scissors

Patterns

> **note**
>
> Cut the faux fur outdoors because it will shed the fibers.

> **note**
>
> The leather used for the handles is a heavier jacket weight. If using a softer leather or suede, consider using two layers or adjust the handle casing measurement.

prepare

1. Cut, as follows:

- one faux fur piece of pattern #TWELVE-1* (bag body)
- one cotton lining piece of pattern #TWELVE-1 (lining)
- one fleece piece of pattern #TWELVE-1 (lining)
- 10" x 4" cotton lining piece (pocket)
- 10" cotton lining square (pocket)
- 2" x 35" leather strip (trim)
- two 2" x 18" leather strips (handles)

*When cutting the faux fur, snip carefully with sharp scissors from the back. Make shallow snips and just cut through the fabric, not the fur, so the fur remains intact.

> **note**
>
> This one-piece pattern was developed specifically for specialty fabrics or fabrics with designs that require less interruption with seams.

2. When finished cutting one piece of fur from pattern #TWELVE-1, trim the fur away from the ½" seam allowances, as shown in Figure 4-102. Use sharp scissors and cut close to the fabric. The seam allowances are across the top, across the bottom, and the two side seams. Do this outside over a large bag to contain the long fibers.

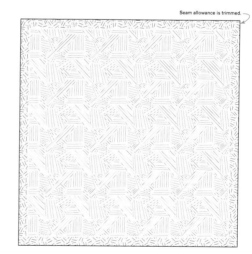

Seam allowance is trimmed.

Figure 4-102

pocket

1. Copy the markings for the 10" strip onto the wrong side of the cotton lining piece for pattern #2. Copy the markings for the pocket onto the wrong side of the cotton lining piece from pattern #1.

2. Place the 10" strip on the lining with right sides together. Sew around the lines.

3. Make a slit inside and clip the curves. Turn the strip through the opening to the wrong side of the lining. Press.

4. From the back, sew to the lining with a ¼" seam allowance from the edge of the strip.

(continued)

zipper

1. Place the zipper under the finished pocket opening. Pin around the opening though all layers and the zipper layer.

2. Use the zipper foot and make any necessary adjustments on your sewing machine to sew the zipper. Start at the short end at the bottom of the zipper and go all the way around, as in Figure 4-103.

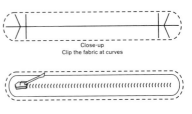

Close-up
Clip the fabric at curves

Figure 4-103

assemble

1. Place the right side of the 10" square of cotton lining on the wrong side of the cotton lining, as shown in Figure 4-104. Sew all around the square ¼" in from the edge all around the square.

2. Fold the lining in half with right sides together. Sew the seam with a ½" seam allowance. Trim to ¼" and press the seams open. Sew across the bottom, trim, and press the seams open.

3. Fold the corners, measure down 2", and sew across. Tack the points, facing toward the center, to the bag.

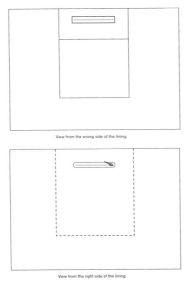

View from the wrong side of the lining.

View from the right side of the lining.

Figure 4-104

4. Switch to a ballpoint sewing machine needle.

5. Fold the fur in half with right sides together. Sew the seam with a ½" seam allowance. Trim seams to ¼" and press the seams open. Sew across the bottom with a ½" seam allowance, trim, and press the seams open.

6. Fold the corners, measure down 2", and sew across.

7. Turn right-side out.

8. Place the lining inside the fur bag with wrong sides together. Match the back seam and pin around the opening at the top.

trim

1. Place the leather trim along the top edge of the bag with the right side of the leather and the fur together. Start at the center back seam. Use clothespins or paperclips to keep in place. When returning to the starting point, overlap the edge ½".

2. With a leather needle attached and topstitch thread in the sewing machine, use a longer stitch length to sew with a ½" seam allowance. Keep the leather and fur layers "taut" by holding on to all layers in front and back of the needle as you are feeding it through the sewing machine. Do not trim the seam.

3. Fold the leather over all the seam allowances to the inside of the bag, as in Figure 4-105. Place the edge lower than the seam line in the front.

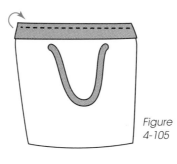

Figure 4-105

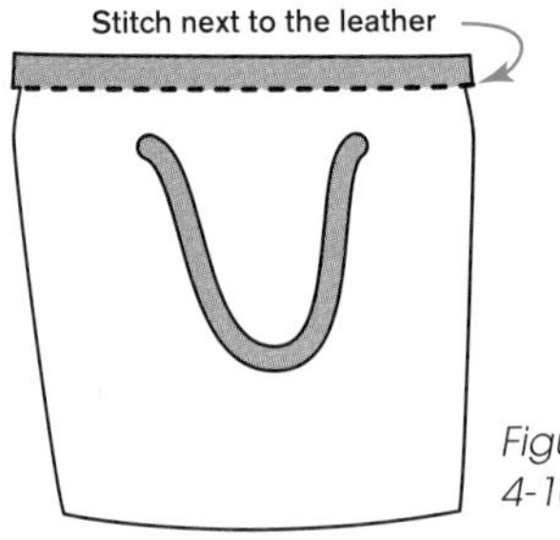

Stitch next to the leather

Figure 4-106

4. Using your zipper foot, topstitch close to the seam line on the front of the bag, as shown in Figure 4-106, making sure to catch the leather on the inside of the bag.

handles

1. Place four pins on the front and back of the bag to mark where the handles will go. Fold the leather strips in half lengthwise with wrong sides together and pin with clothespins or paperclips.

2. Sew with a ⅜" seam, leaving 1" of the handle unsewn at each end. Backstitch at the beginning and end of the seam. Repeat for the other handle.

3. Trim about ¼" of the seam away for each handle and work the plastic tubing inside the leather handle tubes, as shown in Figure 4-107.

4. Part the fur and position one end of a handle. Sew across the bottom of the handle, turn, and sew again, returning to the beginning of the stitches. Repeat for the remaining handle ends.

Figure 4-107

Obi Orange
Blossom

This bag was created to showcase an obi panel. The obi is the cummerbund-like belt worn over a Japanese kimono (see one in the photo on page XX). This one was a very old and special obi. The design and metallic threads are woven into the fabric. The finished width of the obi is 12" and it was just too beautiful to cut. By using this pattern, the obi panel could be framed with orange dupioni and accented with black braid. Three rows of black braid sewn side-by-side separate the panel and the silk. The orange silk dupioni is quilted with meandering lines of the same braid. Black faux lacquer bamboo handles finished the elegant look of the bag. The bag is lined with a fine black cotton fabric, described by the manufacturer as the "blackest black."

finished size

13½" x 15"

fabric and notions

17"-long obi or ½-yard fabric

½-yard orange dupioni silk

½-yard black cotton lining

Tear-away stabilizer

Air-Lite batting

Fusbile web

2 black faux lacquer bamboo handles

3 yards black rayon braid

2 sheets quilting paper

Sewing thread to match the obi

Decorative black rayon thread

Spray adhesive

Fasturn

Pins

Scissors

Patterns

Figure 4-108

prepare

1. Cut, as follows:
   - one orange dupioni silk piece of pattern #TWELVE-1 (bag body)
   - one black cotton lining piece of pattern #TWELVE-1 (lining)
   - two batting pieces of pattern #TWELVE-1
   - one stabilizer piece of pattern #TWELVE-1
   - 2" x 12" black cotton strip
   - 17"-long fabric substitute piece (if you don't have an obi)
   - fusible web piece to match size of obi (or fabric substitute)

embellish

1. Thread the sewing machine with the black rayon thread and set up for free-motion sewing.
2. Follow the meandering design on the black cotton.
3. When finished, tear away the quilting paper.
4. Do the same for the orange silk dupioni.

2. Trace the meandering quilt design from the pattern page onto two sheets of quilting paper.
3. Spray adhesive on the wrong side of the orange dupioni silk, place on the batting, and smooth down evenly.
4. Spray adhesive on the wrong side of the black cotton lining, place on the batting, and smooth down evenly.
5. Place one sheet of quilting paper on the silk and lining pieces and pin in place.

5. Place the tear-away stabilizer under the silk dupioni-batting piece and pin through all layers.
6. Pin the black rayon braid on the meandering stitch line. Pin in place, making sure to "ease" in sufficient braid so it does not pull and "cup" the fabric. Baste in place by hand before cutting off the remainder of the braid.
7. Sew slowly through the center of the braid, as shown in Figure 4-108.
8. When the panel is completed as in the accompanying photo, carefully tear away the stabilizer. Tear along the thread line and the other side will come away easily. Remove the basting stitches.

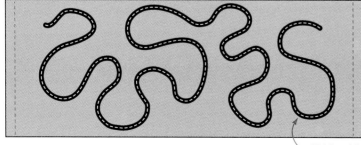

Right side of fabric

Stitch through the middle of the braid.

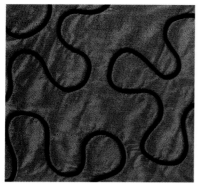

Finish the panel by removing the basting stitches from the braided area.

9. Sew the two side panels with right sides together with a ½" seam allowance. Trim the excess batting from the seam and press open.

10. Turn right-side out.

11. Place the adhesive side of the fusible web on the wrong side of the obi. Press, using a Teflon sheet. When cool, remove the paper backing.

12. Place the panel in the center (use the seam line to mark the center) of the orange silk dupioni silk and pin in place, then press.

13. Pin one row of black braid along the inside edge of the panel. Baste in place. Pin another row of braid on either side of that braid and baste in place. Then, pin and sew third row.

14. Sew through the center of the braids. Do the same for the other side of the panel. Lightly press, using a pressing sheet.

assemble

1. Turn the silk dupioni piece with the wrong side out and then fold in half with right sides together. Pin and sew the seam across the bottom with a ½" seam allowance. Trim the batting from the seams and press open. Fold the corners, measure 2" down, and sew across.

2. Turn right-side out.

3. Fold the black cotton lining in half with right sides together, pin, and sew the side seam with a ½" seam allowance. Trim the batting from the seam and press open. Sew across the bottom leaving a 7" opening in the center. Trim and press the seam open.

loops

1. Fold the strip of black cotton in half lengthwise with right sides together. Sew with a ½" seam allowance.

2. Turn right-side out with a Fasturn and finger-press the seam to one side.

3. Cut into 3" lengths.

4. Fold each length in half and pin.

5. Place a pin in the center front and at the back center seam. Measure the distance between the handle and divide by two. Use that measurement to pin mark on either side of the center pins. Remove the center pins.

6. Place a loop at each mark. The raw edges of the loop should align with the top edge of the bag. Baste in place, as shown in Figure 4-109.

Figure 4-109

7. Place the orange silk dupioni bag inside the cotton lining bag with right sides together, as shown in Figure 4-110. Pin around the top and sew with a ½" seam allowance. Trim to ¼" and cut away the excess batting from the seams.

Figure 4-110

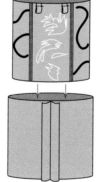

7. Turn right-side out through the 7" opening, as shown in Figure 4-111. Slipstitch to close the opening. Fold the lining to the inside and press the top edge of the bag.

8. For the handles, unscrew the hardware, place the U-shape through the loop, and then place the handle between the hardware and replace the screw.

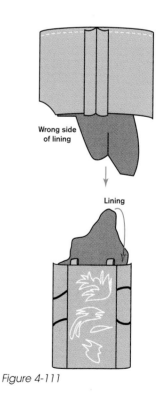

Wrong side of lining

Lining

Figure 4-111

Marrakesh Tapestry Tote

This upholstery weight tapestry with lively monkeys was perfect for embellishing with green silk dupioni as a background for the coconut buttons and brown silk dupioni for the Asian coins. Each side of the bag is adorned with a different embellishment. Who said you had to make up your mind?

finished size

13" x 12"

fabric and notions

½-yard monkey tapestry

⅔-yard green dupioni silk

¼-yard brown dupioni silk

Air-Lite batting

9 1"coconut buttons

5 Asian coins

15" black rayon braid

2 5" bamboo handles

Sewing thread to match fabrics

Decorative variegated polyester embroidery or rayon thread

Spray adhesive

Pins

Scissors

Patterns

note

This wonderfully shaped bamboo handle adds a lot of interest to the bag. The size is determined by measuring the distance between the center of each curl. The handle used for this bag pattern is a 5" handle. If your handle is larger in width, just cut the pattern in half down the center and add the difference. The markings for the coins and buttons will then need to be adjusted.

prepare

1. Cut, as follows:
- two monkey tapestry pieces of pattern #THIRTEEN-1 (bag body)
- two green dupioni silk pieces of pattern #THIRTEEN-1 (lining)
- two batting pieces of pattern #THIRTEEN-1 (lining)
- four batting pieces of pattern #THIRTEEN-2 (bottom strip)
- one brown dupioni silk piece of pattern #THIRTEEN-2 (bottom strip)
- one green dupioni silk piece of pattern #THIRTEEN-2 (bottom strip)

embellish

1. Thread the sewing machine with a variegated decorative thread and set up for free-motion sewing. Free-motion sew with meandering lines or your favorite quilting design on all four green dupioni silk pieces.

2. Use free-motion on the green dupioni silk strip and then sew on the coconut shell buttons, as shown in Figure 4-112.

2. Mark the placement for the five buttons on the green dupioni silk strip and the coins for the brown dupioni silk.

3. Spray adhesive on the wrong side of four pieces of green silk and place on the batting. Smooth evenly.

4. Spray adhesive on the wrong side of brown and green dupioni silk strips and place on the batting. Smooth evenly.

3. Use the markings on the brown dupioni silk strip to place the Asian coins and loops. Place the coins through the loops, fold in half, and baste in place ½" from the top edge, as shown in Figure 4-113.

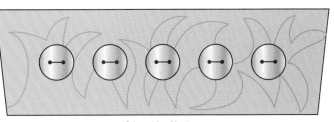

Figure 4-112   **Other side of bottom**

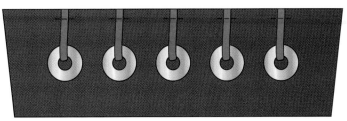

Figure 4-113

assemble

1. Sew the brown strip to one of the monkey tapestry pieces with right sides together, matching notches, as in Figure 4-114.

2. Sew the green strip to the other monkey tapestry piece with right sides together, matching notches. Press the seams toward the silk.

3. Sew the green silk dupioni body pieces to the strips.

4. Referring to Figure 4-115, place the two tapestry/silk pieces with right sides together, pin, and sew the top seam with a ½" seam allowance. Do not trim the tapestry fabric or press the seams open. Now, sew across the bottom and then press the seams toward the side with the brown silk strip.

5. Turn right-side out.

6. Place the two quilted green silk lining pieces with right sides together, pin, and sew the side seams with a ½" seam allowance. Trim seams to ¼" and trim away the excess batting. Press the seams open. Sew across the bottom leaving a 5" opening. Trim and press the seam open.

7. Place the tapestry bag inside the green silk lining bag with right sides together. Match the side seams and pin around the perimeter of the top of the bag. Sew around the perimeter with a ½" seam allowance. Sew another line of

stitching right next to the first within the seam allowance. Trim the seam allowance to slightly more than ¼" and clip the curves up to the seam lines, being careful not to cut through the seams.

8. Turn the bag right-side out through the opening and slipstitch to close.

Figure 4-114

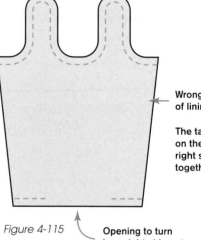

Wrong side of lining

The tapestry is on the inside, right sides together (RST)

Figure 4-115

Opening to turn bag right side out

attach the handle

1. Fold each curved tab over the curled area of the handles.

2. Fold each tab over 2½" and pin.

3. Sew a coconut button in the curve of each tab. Use black thread to sew the button on so it will not show after sewing through all layers, including the tapestry fabric.

Coconut shell buttons, Asian coins, and monkeys with umbrellas conspire to create a charming vignette—or two.

Night and Day

This reversible bag with strips of black and white fabric is lined with an animal print and embellished with swinging black tassels. It'll take you from the office to dinner on the town in one turn.

finished size
11" x 15"

fabric and notions

½-yard each of eight coordinating black-and-white cotton print fabrics

½-yard black cotton fabric

⅔-yard cotton animal print

⅔-yard white cotton

Air-Lite batting

2 5" bamboo handles

8 black tassels

2 sheets tear-away stabilizer

Sewing thread that best blends with your fabric colors

Decorative rayon or variegated polyester machine embroidery thread

Measuring tape

Spray adhesive

Fasturn

Pins

Scissors

Patterns

prepare

1. Cut, as follows:
- two 2" x 26" bias strips of each of the eight black-and-white coordinating cotton fabrics (bag body; 16 total strips)
- two animal print pieces of pattern # FOURTEEN-1 (lining)
- two white cotton pieces of pattern # FOURTEEN-1 (base)
- four batting pieces of pattern # FOURTEEN-1 (lining)
- 2" x 21" black cotton bias strip (trim)
- 2" x 12" black cotton bias strip (loops)

2. Spray adhesive on the wrong side of both of the animal print lining pieces, place on the batting, and smooth down evenly.

3. Spray adhesive on the wrong side of the white cotton, place on the batting, and smooth down evenly.

4. Place a sheet of tear away stabilizer under each of the two white cotton-batting pieces and pin in place. This will be the base for the application of the black and white strips of fabric.

5. Place the first black strip along the top edge of the base piece, with the edge of the black fabric 2" to the left of the beginning of base edge, as shown in Figure 4-116. This is so the bottom edge of the black strip will cover the base. Pin to the top edge and cut off the excess fabric, always checking to cover the base.

Figure 4-116

6. Sew the top edge of the strip to the base with a ¼" seam allowance, as in Figure 4-117.

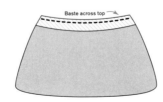

Figure 4-117

7. Referring to Figure 4-118, place the next strip with right sides together at the bottom edge of the first black strip. Once again, start the second strip 2" before the black strip. The second strip will be facing up. Ease the strip loosely, pinning ¼" from the edge. Flip the second piece down to see if you have eased it enough. If it tends to curl under, it will need more ease. In that case, remove the strip and try again. Also, check to see if the bottom of the second strip covers the base sides.

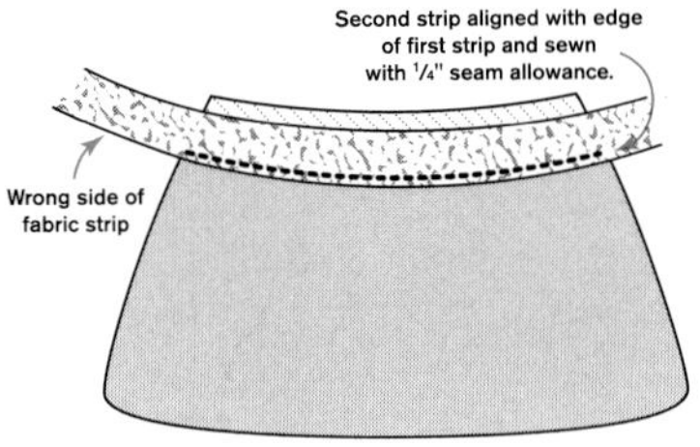

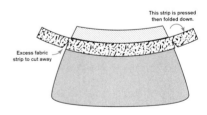

Figure 4-118

8. Now sew rows 1 and 2 with a ¼" seam allowance through all layers. Use the mini iron to press the seam, flip the second strip down, as in Figure 4-119, and press the second strip and seams down.

Figure 4-119

9. Continue in this manner, as Figure 4-120 shows the next piece added, until you have completed all eight rows. Sew the last strip edge down ¼" from the base edge.

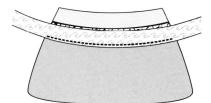

Figure 4-120

10. Tear away the stabilizer. Repeat for the other side of the bag.

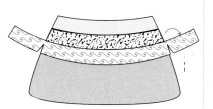

embellish

1. Thread the sewing machine with decorative thread and set up for free-motion sewing. Use meandering lines or your favorite quilting pattern to quilt the lining fabric and batting.
2. For the loops, fold the 12" black cotton strip in half lengthwise with right sides together and stitch with ¼" seam allowance.
3. Turn the strip right-side out with the Fasturn and finger-press with the seams to the side.
4. Cut the tube into 3" lengths. Fold each tube in half and pin.

assemble

1. Place the two pieced units with right sides together. Match the strips at the side seams. Pin. Sew the sides with a ½" seam allowance. Sew another line of stitching right next to the first within the seam allowance for reinforcement. Trim the seams to ¼" and press the seams to one side. Sew across the bottom with a ¼" seam allowance. Press to the same side. Turn right-side out.
2. Place the two quilted lining pieces with right sides together, pin, and sew the side seams with a ½" seam allowance. Trim the seams to ¼" and cut away the excess batting. Press the seams to one side, in the opposite direction as the pieced bag. Sew across the bottom with a ¼" seam allowance.

3. Place the lining bag inside the pieced bag, as shown in Figure 4-121. Match the side seams and pin the two bags together around the top edge.

Figure 4-121

4. Place a pin in the center of the front and back.
5. Measure the width of the handle (in this case, 5") and divide that width number in half (2½").
6. Measure 2½" to each side of the center marking pins and mark with pins. Remove the center pins.
7. Place a loop at each side pin. The raw edges of the loops should align with the top of the bag. Baste them in place.

trim

1. Measure around the opening of the bag ¼" down from the edge. Add ½" to that measurement for seams.
2. Cut the 21" black cotton strip to that measurement. Fold the strip with right sides together and sew the two short ends with a ¼" seam. Press the seam open.
3. Place the strip around the opening of the bag with right sides together. Match the seam of the

black strip to one of the side seams of the bag, pin, and sew with a ¼" seam.
4. Fold the black strip over the seams to the inside of the bag, as shown in Figure 4-122. Fold the edge under to create a ½"-wide trim.

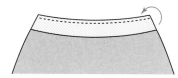

Figure 4-122

5. Bring that folded edge to the stitching line on the inside of the bag, as in Figure 4-123.

View from inside

6. Slipstitch or stitch-in-the-ditch to finish the trim.
7. Add handles and embellish with a swinging tassel to each side of each handle piece.

Travel Tokyo

This purse allows you to carry a little history along on your travels. Vintage kimono strips are stunning when matched with a strip of cotton velveteen. Adding more strips, longer strips, or a larger black velvet trim can easily enlarge this bag.

finished size

7½" x 10"

fabric and notions

⅓-yard black cotton

⅛-yard black cotton velveteen

½-yard vintage kimono fabric

Air-Lite batting

4" black rayon braid

1 set of magnetic snaps

Iron-on nylon tricot stabilizer

Bamboo toggle

Sewing thread to match fabric

2 4" bamboo handles

Spray adhesive

Pins

Scissors

Patterns

note

Patterns cut from velvet and velveteen should be cut facing the same direction (with the nap) because of the surface texture. Cutting the fabric in two different directions will result in a two-toned bag because the light hits the nap differently. Velvet and velveteen should be pressed from the wrong side to avoid crushing the nap.

prepare

1. Cut, as follows:
- two black cotton pieces of pattern # FIFTEEN-1 (lining)
- four black cotton velveteen pieces of pattern # FIFTEEN-2 (trim)
- eight 2" x 17" kimono fabric strips (bag body)
- 2" x 12" black cotton strip (loops)
- two 3" stabilizer squares

2. Mark the placement for the magnetic snap on two of the black velveteen pieces. Press the iron on stabilizer on the wrong side of the fabric to stabilize the area.

3. Carefully, cut two small slits and send the magnetic snap prongs through. Bend the prongs to the side. Do the same for the other snap.

4. Spray adhesive on the wrong side of the other two black velveteen pieces, place on the batting, and smooth evenly.

strips

1. Sew the strips together with ¼" seam allowances. Press all the seams to one side, all facing the same direction.

2. Place the pieced kimono strip on the batting piece of similar size.

3. Set the sewing machine for free-motion. Using decorative thread with sewing thread of the same color in the bobbin, create a meandering stitch to quilt the two layers together. Use a large, loose design so it will not detract from the beautiful motifs on the fabric.

loops

1. Fold the 12" strip of black cotton in half lengthwise, with right sides together. Sew with a ½" seam allowance.

2. Turn right-side out with a Fasturn and finger-press with the seam to the side.

3. Cut into 3" lengths, fold each length in half, and pin.

4. Place pins at the center of the top edge of each black velveteen piece with the snap placement.

5. Measure the width of the handle (in this case, 4"). Divide the measurement in half (2").

6. Mark 2" on either side of both pins. Remove the center pins. Place the loops where marked. The raw edges of the loops should align with the edge of the velveteen. Pin and baste in place.

4. Cut away the excess batting.

5. Set your machine for a longer stitch length (about eight to nine stitches per inch). Sew a row of stitches ½" from the edge of the strip-pieced kimono piece, leaving 4" long thread tails at the beginning and the end. Do not backstitch. Then, sew another row of stitches ¼" from the edge in the seam allowance.

(continued)

Carry a bit of the orient with you always.

note

Don't forget to use your mini iron.

assemble

1. Fold the black velveteen/strip-pieced piece in half with right sides together. Sew the side seams with a ½" seam allowance. Be sure to match seams where the velveteen is sewn to the strip-pieced fabric. Do not trim the side seam. Press seams open. Turn right-side out.

2. Sew the two velveteen pieces with the magnetic snaps to the black cotton lining pieces.

3. Place the two black cotton lining pieces with right sides together. Pin. Sew the side seams with a ½" seam allowance. Trim to ¼" and press the seams open. Sew across the bottom, leaving a 5" opening at the center to turn. Trim seams and press open.

4. Place the velveteen/strip-pieced fabric bag inside the lining bag with right sides together. Pin around the opening and sew with a ½" seam allowance. Trim seam to ¼".

5. Turn the bag right-side out through the opening. Slipstitch the opening closed.

6. Push the lining inside the bag and press around the opening from the lining side to achieve the look of Figure 4-126.

6. Referring to Figure 4-124, pull two threads from the wrong side of the fabric and pull slowly with your left hand. With your right hand, carefully and slowly pull the fabric in the opposite direction, gathering the fabric to the middle. Repeat the gathering process from the other end. Gather until the fabric is a 9" width. Disperse the gathers evenly. Do the same for the other end.

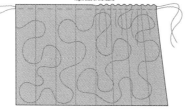

Figure 4-124

Figure 4-126

trim

1. Thread the rayon braid through the bamboo toggle loop and place on the black velveteen trim, as shown in Figure 4-125. Remember, this is the bottom edge of the trim that will be sewn to the strip pieced fabric, opposite the handle loops.

2. Place the velveteen piece to the strip-pieced fabric with right sides together. With the strip-pieced side facing you, pin together.

3. Sew along the ½" gathering seam line. Do the same for the other end. Don't forget, the rayon loop and toggle should be sewn into one of these seams.

handle

1. Remove the screw from each side of the handle.

2. Place the hardware through each loop and replace the screw.

Figure 4-125

This black-and-white showstopper by Jeaniene Dibble is finished with a black beaded handle and bead trim.

Gail Sahara's black silk purse is embellished with Japanese ribbons and metallic ribbon anchored with Victorian glass buttons.

"Gaugin," by Lindsay Hager, is a bag that's hand-woven on a triangle loom with hand-dyed wool, viscose, cotton and silk, with hand-twisted cord.

This plaid and solid silk dupioni bag by Sarah Hochhauser's is embellished with beaded fringe and bamboo handles.

Sarah Hochhauser's quilted silk purse is festooned with hand-dyed silk trim and handle.

In "I've Got the Blues," Lindsay Hager incorporates torn silk strips woven with yarn and ribbon, silk lining, hand-twisted cord of yarn and metallic thread.

Lindsay Hager's "Twill Me" is a loom-woven creation using hand-dyed rayon warp, rayon and metallic weft, silk lining, mother-of-pearl fish button, and hand-twisted cord.

"Shades of the Sixties" by Lindsay Hager was hand-woven on a triangle loom using hand-dyed ribbon with metallic edges, silk lining, and hand-twisted cord.

Cotton ticking with topstitching gives this purse by Pauline House its upbeat, informal appeal.

Floral cotton with braid trim and vintage shell button make up the beautiful components of this bag by Gail Sahara.

Resources

Air-Lite® Bond Tight Batting
(800) 521-1267 (wholesale only)
Polyester and cotton battings.

Beacon™ Company
(800) TO CRAFT (800) 862-7238
Fabri-Tac™, Liqui-Fuse™,
and Gem-Tac™

Bernina
www.berninausa.com
Sewing machines and
accessories.

Brother
www.brother.com
Sewing machines and
accessories.

DYEnamic Fabrics
www.DYEnamicFabrics.com
Batik yardage, patterns, and kits.

Fabric.com
www.fabric.com

Gail Sahara
www.gailsahara@yahoo.com
Vintage buttons and jewelry.

Ghee's
www.ghees.com
(318) 226-1701
Purse patterns, hardware, chain straps,
and books.

Haberman Fabrics
www.habermanfabrics.com
(248) 541-0010
Fashion, quilting, and decorator
fabrics.

Hartsdale Fabrics
www.hartsdalefabrics.com
(914) 428-7780
Fashion, quilting, and decorator
fabrics, purse handles, trims, and faux
fur.

HTC Fusible Fleece
(770) 723-0300 (wholesale only)
Craft fleece.

Husqvarna Viking
www.husqvarnaviking.com
Sewing machines and
accessories.

Indonesian Batiks
www.indobatiks.com
(360) 299-3968
Batik art panels and yardage.

Jacquard
www.jacquardproducts.com
(800) 442-0455 (wholesale only)
Lumiere fabric paints.

Jackman Fabrics
www.jackmanfabrics.com
(800) 758-3742
Fashion, quilting, and decorator
fabrics, purse handles, and trims.

Janome
www.janome.com
Sewing machines and
accessories.

Kai Scissors
www.kaiscissors.com
(800) 481-4943

Kimono My Home
eebart@aldelphia.net
Vintage kimono, buttons, and textiles.

Krause Publications
www.krause.com
(888) 457-2873

Laura Murray
www.lauramurraydesigns.com
(612) 825-1209
Specialty vintage kimonos.

Maeda Importing
www.maedaimporting.com
(407) 302-7172
Furoshiki, Japanese brocade, and
gifts.

Rama
emeraldstacey@hotmail.com
Handmade raku buttons.

Revisions (Diane Ericson)
www.revisions-ericson.com
Patterns, stencils, and books.

Richland Silk Company
www.richlandsilk.com
(517) 263-4756
Silk batting.

Sara Elizabeth
shochhauser@aol.com
Books and patterns.

*A final inspirational gallery piece
created by Sarah Hochhauser.*

Sew Contempo
www.sewcontempo.com
(281) 333-5320
Fashion, sewing, and quilting fabrics.

Sewing Studio
www.sewing.net
(800) 831-1492
Fashion, quilting, decorator and bridal
fabrics, leather, beaded fringe,
feather fringe, and purse handles and
hardware.

South Beach Trimmings
www.southbeachtrimmings.com
(800) 859-1651
Beaded trims, leather, buttons, braids

Stephanie Masae Kimura
P.O. Box 1471
Jensen Beach, FL 34958
www.kimurapatterns.com
Patterns, embellishment, fabrics, kits,
and books.

The Quilted Dragon
www.quilted-dragon.com
(253) 582-7455
Furoshiki, raku buttons

The Leather Factory
www.leatherfactory.com

The Warm Company
www.warmcompany.com
Cotton batting and fusible
polyester fleece.

Tsukineko
www.tsukineko.com
(800) 769-6693 (wholesale only)
Stamp pads, and Kanji stencils.

Yoko Trading
www.yokodana.com
(610) 987-9710
Kimonos, fabrics, and antiques.